BRINGING HEAVEN TO EARTH

LIVING THE PROCESS OF SANCTIFICATION

BEACON & QUILL
PUBLISHING LLC.

DAVID POWELL

"Truthful, practical, and challenging—yet full of grace. These are the words that come to mind as I read "Bringing Heaven to Earth".

Drawing from his own journey marked by personal disappointments and hard-earned lessons, David invites us into a transformative path of surrender to the Holy Spirit, a deeper understanding of God's love, and the sanctifying process of becoming more like Christ.

When David writes, "I now see sanctification not as a requirement to perform, but as an invitation to be healed and transformed", he summarizes why we need this book. It's a strong invitation to resist the temptation of striving for perfection. Instead, it encourages us to rest in God's perfect grace—a grace that liberates us from the exhausting pursuit of "never enough."

With clear, step-by-step reasoning, the book is both accessible and deeply rooted in Scripture. It offers profound insights without overwhelming the reader, making it suitable for believers at any stage of their walk.

Whether read individually or studied in a group setting, its message has the potential to inspire, convict, and renew."

Pier Francesco Abortivi
International Director of Adventive Cross Cultural Initiatives

"David Powell writes with a refreshing vulnerability that is rare in Christian writing. His story is approachable and honest, prompting readers from every stage of faith to see the beauty of walking with God in process. Bringing Heaven to Earth invites us to consider sanctification not as a burden to bear, but as a journey to delight in."

Eva Cosby, Missions Leader and Mentor to Young Adults

"In my 15 years of counseling, I have often found myself sitting with those who struggle to come near to God because they believe they need to have it all together or they can't be honest with God. This book is a gentle guide that unlocks this stuck place in faith, revealing and leading us to God's truth, His desire to be with us, not to perform for Him. David shares biblical truths and his personal story to connect us to God's transformation, intimacy, and fulfillment for our lives in Christ."

Tina M. Salvatierra, L.C.S.W., Owner & Counselor of Reveal to Heal Counseling

"Believers at all points in their spiritual walk can benefit from the wisdom and discernment that Powell shares in this book. Bringing Heaven to Earth is a gift obtained through perseverance and hope that will surely bring transformation to the body of Christ."

Caleb Earle, Field Director, Global Year

"As a pastor, preacher and lover of the Bible, I feel the author has redisplayed the Word of God for me, topically, through the lens of the theology of sanctification. It is as if he asked scholars to reorder the presentation of God's Word to explain sanctification. The topic literally unfolds scripture by scripture. It is that organized, thorough and clear. This is exactly the kind of tool a pastor wants every new believer to read. However, most Christians have never heard this message so clearly and with such biblical support. Therefore, it is the kind of tool a pastor wants everyone in his community to read and absorb."

John Mullen, Senior Pastor at Prague Christian Fellowship

More books from

BEACON & QUILL PUBLISHING LLC.

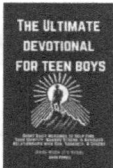 Find Your True Identity in Christ, Strengthen Your Faith, and Face Life's Challenges with Confidence – All in Just a Few Minutes a Day with This 52-Week Devotional

 Support the teen boy in your life as he navigates faith, identity, and life's challenges with The Companion Guide for Parents & Mentors to The Ultimate Devotional for Teen Boys.

 This 5-day meditation devotional is designed for busy men who want to grow spiritually without feeling overwhelmed.

 Whether a young person in your life is moving out for the first time, trying to manage money, or learning to navigate awkward adult conversations, this book breaks it all down into practical, bite-sized lessons—with a dose of humor to keep them engaged.

BEACON & QUILL
PUBLISHING LLC.

Library of Congress Control Number: 2025915829

First published 2025 in Colorado Springs, Colorado, USA

Author: David Powell

Editors: Sarah Powell, Meghan Ward

eBook ISBN: 978-1-967850-18-1

Paperback ISBN: 978-1-967850-19-8

Hardback ISBN: 978-1-967850-20-4

CONTENTS

Introduction:

A Work in Progress

The day after my wife and I got married, we packed up our lives and moved to Mexico. We were young, in love, and eager to serve God. We landed in a small town called Chapala and, over the next twelve years, we spent eight years living in Mexico. We returned to the U.S. only to have our three children before heading back across the border. Our journey eventually led us to serve in Honduras, Belize, Italy, Greece, and the Czech Republic. We experienced incredible miracles and walked through deep valleys. We preached the gospel, prayed for the sick, fed the poor, and discipled believers; and yet, I often felt like a fraud.

Even while doing all the "right" things, there were moments when I sat down to pray and thought, *"Why am I even a missionary? I don't think I love people the way I'm supposed to. In fact, sometimes they really annoy me."* That might sound harsh, but it was my honest reality. It's not that I never loved people, but the struggle to love well often felt bigger than I was capable of handling. I tried to be the perfect Christ-like example, but I wrestled internally with lust, fear of man, and insecurity. Sometimes I felt like a hypocrite, but I never felt free to talk about it.

There was a silent expectation that I should have it all together. I feared that if I admitted my struggles, I might lose financial support or credibility. People might stop respecting my teaching. So I put on a smile, kept preaching, kept leading, and kept my doubts and fears tucked away. I tried even harder to appear righteous, to say and do the "right" things. My teaching often brought condemnation instead of encouragement, as I used Scripture to chastise people for making poor choices. I emphasized what the listeners needed "to do," instead of helping them grow in relationship with a loving Father. For thirty years my spiritual life was a rollercoaster, filled with moments of passionate faith, followed by moments of deep discouragement and the nagging sense that I wasn't measuring up.

Everything began to shift when I turned fifty.

My wife and I were preparing to move to the Czech Republic and we were struggling to walk in unity with this decision, which was creating several difficult conversations. During that season, I had one of the most honest conversations I've ever had with God. I told Him plainly, *"I don't know how to love You with all my heart, soul, mind, and strength. I don't even know what that practically looks like. And I certainly don't know how to love others well. Please... teach me."* That simple, vulnerable prayer opened a door.

What followed was a journey of inner healing and sanctification unlike anything I had experienced in the previous decades of ministry. God began answering that prayer in powerful, personal ways. One of the first turning points came through a dream.

After a misunderstanding with my wife one evening, I had a strange dream. In the dream, we were sitting side-by-side and watching some kind of performance, when suddenly my arms and legs began flailing uncontrollably. I looked up and saw a demon holding marionette strings, jerking me around like a puppet. But I wasn't angry at the demon; I was upset that my wife didn't even notice what was happening to me. I woke up disturbed, but I wasn't quite sure what it meant.

The next day, I hiked up a mountain to be alone with God. After a long climb, I sat on a rock, feeling exhausted, and asked, *"Okay, God, what was that dream about?"* In that moment, I felt the Holy Spirit bring a series of memories before my mind's eye, starting from when I was just three years old, all the way to the present. Scene after scene of rejection. Then I heard Him speak, not audibly, but clearly in my spirit: *"You are fighting a Spirit of Rejection. And you can't win a spiritual battle in your flesh."*

It hit me like a lightning bolt. I realized that years of fighting anxious thoughts, quoting Scripture, trying to "take every thought captive" - it hadn't been enough. This was a spiritual battle, and it needed a spiritual weapon. The night before, my wife had just been sharing some of her emotions, but I had heard those emotions through a filter of rejection. This then caused me to react with defensive walls of protection and judgment. She knew nothing of my internal struggle (honestly, I didn't either); she was simply stating how she felt at the moment.

Right there on that mountain, I asked God to forgive me for agreeing with that Spirit of Rejection. I forgave everyone who had rejected me, just as He had shown me in the slideshow of memories. And I renounced and cast off that spirit in Jesus' name. Immediately, I felt lighter. My wife noticed the change in me the moment I got home.

Since that day, I've recognized those old thoughts more quickly. When they try to creep in—those feelings of being unwanted or mis-understood—I see them for what they are and dismiss them before they can take root. This freedom was not something I could have manufactured. It came only by the power of the Holy Spirit. I didn't even know what was wrong until God revealed it to me.

I used to be so judgmental, thinking other people were the ones who needed to change. However, through this process, God began to show me my own brokenness and His love for me in the midst of it. It softened me. It made me love Him more. As I saw His patience with me, I began to extend that same grace to others.

I now see sanctification not as a requirement to perform, but as an invitation to be healed and transformed. I've stopped expecting people to already be who they're becoming. I no longer carry the pressure to perform or appear perfect. Instead, I've learned to be vulnerable. I've found that in sharing my real process, I've helped others far more than when I tried to put on a flawless front. I've gone from being an excellent Pharisee to an imperfect, but loved and accepted, follower of Jesus.

God even showed me that Jesus, our perfect Savior, modeled vulnerability. He left all the glory of heaven, angelic worship, complete order, and perfect peace, to become a fragile, dependent baby in a manger. That's vulnerability. Why would we expect to follow Him without also stepping into that kind of honest humility?

In these past few years, I've found more freedom than I did in the fifty years before. One passage that brought it all into focus for me was Hebrews 4. Verses 10 and 11 stunned me: *"Anyone who enters God's rest also rests from their works, just as God did from His. Let us, therefore, make every effort to enter that rest..."* I realized I had been laboring to be perfect when Scripture tells us to labor to enter into His rest.

I heard the Holy Spirit gently speak to me and say, "As long as you are working to sanctify yourself, I will stand back and wait." The Spirit of God is typically gentle and does not force Himself upon us. But when I began striving to rest, trusting Him instead of myself, then the Spirit took over the work I could have never done on my own.

This book is for people like me. It is for people who love Jesus, but feel stuck; for people who know they're supposed to be changed, but still wrestle with the same old fears, thoughts, and patterns. If that's you, I pray this book lifts the weight of shame off your shoulders. I pray it replaces guilt with grace and that it exposes the performance trap for what it is. Sanctification is a process. You're not behind. You're not disqualified. You're becoming. And the Holy Spirit, not you in your own strength, is the One who will finish the good work that God has begun in you.

At the end, you'll find some "Affirmations of Identity in Christ" and "Group Study Questions" for each chapter. To get the most out of this book and the journey of sanctification, I encourage you to go through it with others. Let's walk this journey together.

PART I:

THE TENSION WE LIVE IN

A missionary friend, who currently serves in Northern Ireland, recently came to visit. We were discussing sanctification and the concept of living in the tension between how God sees us and how we perceive ourselves. She mentioned that she has a picture hanging over her desk of a drill driving a screw into a piece of wood. It is her reminder of the tension we face as we go deeper in the Lord. If we resist the tension, we might break. But if we hold firm in the tension, with the goal in mind, we will indeed be brought closer and deeper to our beautiful Saviour.

Chapter 1

New Creation, Old Habits

"I thought I'd be different."

If you've ever said that, or thought it, after giving your life to Christ, you're not alone. For many of us, salvation brought a powerful moment of change. We felt lighter, forgiven, even new. But over time, old habits crept back in. Anger. Fear. Lust. Insecurity. Pride. Gossip. Apathy. Whatever it was for you, it left you wondering, *"If I'm really a new creation, why do I still struggle with the same things?"* This chapter is for the part of you that feels discouraged by that question, and the part that needs to know the truth of what God says.

The Promise of the New Creation

Let's begin with the verse many of us know by heart:

"Therefore, if anyone is in Christ, the new creation has come: The old has gone, the new is here!" 2 Corinthians 5:17

That's not a maybe. That's a promise. *"If anyone is in Christ..."* You're not disqualified from this verse if you're still struggling. Paul didn't say, "If anyone has achieved perfection..." or "If anyone feels like a new creation..." The only qualification is being in Christ. So why doesn't it always feel true? Because there's a difference between how God sees us and how we currently see or experience ourselves.

God's View vs. Our Reality

God is not limited by time in the way that we are. He sees the end from the beginning. Scripture says:

"I make known the end from the beginning, from ancient times, what is still to come. I say, 'My purpose will stand, and I will do all that I please.'" Isaiah 46:10

God sees us through the finished work of Christ. From His eternal vantage point, your sanctification is already complete. When He looks at you, He sees you as holy and blameless because of Jesus:

"But now he has reconciled you by Christ's physical body through death to present you holy in his sight, without blemish and free from accusation—if you continue in your faith, established and firm, and do not move from the hope held out in the gospel." Colossians 1:22–23a

Yet we live within time. We experience life moment by moment. We are very much in process. The new creation exists, but we're learning how to live in it.

Think of it like a seed. The moment you plant it, the life of the plant is already there. It's real. It's growing. But it will take time, light, water, and care to see what it fully becomes. Your heavenly DNA is present from the moment you believed in Jesus Christ as your saviour (your spiritual birth, being born again), but you must grow and mature from a baby to an adult. Just like epigenetics and the methylation process in your physical body, your environment can either suppress or call out gene expressions in your spiritual DNA (more about this in Chapter 7). You can also think of it like yeast being mixed in dough, as Jesus shared:

"He told them still another parable: 'The kingdom of heaven is like yeast that a woman took and mixed into about sixty pounds of flour until it worked all through the dough.'" Matthew 13:33

Regardless of what you see at this moment, the yeast is working through the dough. His DNA is in the process of making you more like Him.

Why the Struggle Continues

When we don't understand sanctification as a process, we tend to respond to ongoing struggles in a few damaging ways:

1. **We fake it.** We put on a mask and pretend everything's fine, even when we're struggling. This creates hypocrisy and is most damaging to our families, especially our children, who can see the truth.

2. **We feel ashamed.** We assume we must be doing something wrong, or that maybe we aren't really saved. This can cause us to distance ourselves from others we perceive as being "better" than us. This separation causes our growth to slow even more.

3. **We try harder.** We double down on discipline and effort, trying to force transformation through willpower. This leads to frustration and an inner hypocrisy that those close to us can still sense. It also often makes us judgmental of others, as we try to find a sense of confidence and security in our efforts by comparing ourselves to those around us. In our need for grace, we withhold grace from others, damaging

our relationships.

I've done all three. Maybe you have too.

However, the early Christians struggled in similar ways. In Romans 7, Paul himself describes the battle between the flesh and the Spirit:

"I do not understand what I do. For what I want to do I do not do, but what I hate I do... For I have the desire to do what is good, but I cannot carry it out... So I find this law at work: Although I want to do good, evil is right there with me." Romans 7:15,18b,21

Sound familiar?

Paul—who had an encounter with the risen Christ and became the greatest missionary of his time—was still describing an internal war. That doesn't disqualify him. It reveals the honest reality that transformation is an ongoing process. Many believe that in Romans 7, Paul refers to his life before Christ. Yet the principles he outlines still apply to us when we are caught up in religious observance to try and win or earn God's favor. Whether you know Jesus or not, you can be caught in this trap. Paul also writes to the Galatians not to fall into this trap of performance:

"You foolish Galatians! Who has bewitched you? Before your very eyes Jesus Christ was clearly portrayed as crucified. I would like to learn just one thing from you: Did you receive the Spirit by the works of the law, or by believing what you heard? Are you so foolish? After beginning by means of the Spirit, are you now trying to finish by means of the flesh?" Galatians 3:1-3

Sanctification Is Not the Same as Salvation

Salvation is instant. The moment you put your faith in Jesus Christ, you are justified—made right with God—through His blood:

"Therefore, since we have been justified through faith, we have peace with God through our Lord Jesus Christ." Romans 5:1

Sanctification, however, is a process. It is the daily work of the Holy Spirit shaping you into the image of Christ. It involves your cooperation, but depends on His power:

"It is God who works in you to will and to act in order to fulfill his good purpose." Philippians 2:13

You are not left to figure this out alone. But it is a journey, akin to a walk, not a sprint. If you have ever been a parent or teacher, you know that every child learns and matures at a different pace. So it is with us in this spiritual journey. Be patient with yourself and others as we walk this journey at our own pace, prescribed by the Holy Spirit.

Embracing the Journey

The truth is, transformation doesn't happen overnight. Habits don't break instantly. Thought patterns don't rewire in a moment. Emotional wounds don't vanish because we memorized a verse. Our family culture, as well as our national culture, does not just disappear the moment we accept Jesus. Instead, the Spirit leads us, step by step. Scripture calls it "being transformed," in the present tense:

"And we all, who with unveiled faces contemplate the Lord's glory, are being transformed into his image with ever-increasing glory, which comes from the Lord, who is the Spirit." 2 Corinthians 3:18

Did you catch that? *"Being transformed."* Not already perfected. And this transformation comes from *"the Lord, who is the Spirit,"* not from your striving or performance.

A friend shared a story with me about a farmer who lives near them. They heard that some lambs had been born and went to see them. The mother and father sheep were both bright white, but all the lambs had a brownish tint to their coats. When asked, the farmer confidently responded, saying, "You see, there were only the two sheep, but around them are all these brown cows. The sheep end up staring at the cows all day, and it has affected the color of their lambs." That is called epigenetics (more on that in Chapter 7). Think of Jacob getting Laban's flocks and herds in Genesis 30. He stripped pieces of bark from branches and set them in front of the strong cattle, sheep and goats that were about to give birth. This caused them to give birth to spotted and striped offspring, which became his according to the contract he had with Laban. Laban ended up with the weak animals and Jacob with the strong. With this in mind, the more we focus on and observe the Lord's glory, the more we become like Him, as in the verse above!

You're Not Alone

If you've felt discouraged, doubting whether you're really changed... if you've wondered whether you're the only one who still struggles... I want you to hear this:

You are not alone.

Even the apostles had moments of failure. Peter, Paul, Mark, and many others all struggled and made mistakes along the way. The "perfect" people and families you see at church every Sunday are all working through their own struggles and challenges. We've all heard of many Catholic priests and Evangelical leaders who have fallen. If they had learned to be vulnerable and walk in the process of sanctification, maybe their falls could have been from a much lower height with less damage. In fact, instead of harming people, they might have helped people by providing an honest and genuine example to those around them of what it looks like to walk in this process. Instead, they hid their struggles to keep up an appearance and climb higher up the ladder. Remember King Saul and King David. They were both sinners, but Saul always tried to impress people whereas David wanted to please God. As Jesus told the Pharisees, there can be a vast difference between outward appearance and internal condition.

God's Grace Is Big Enough for Your Process

Grace isn't a license to sin; it's the power to keep walking while we're being changed. God doesn't demand perfection before He loves us or uses us. His love is what enables our growth.

"For it is by grace you have been saved, through faith—and this is not from yourselves, it is the gift of God—not by works, so that no one can boast." Ephesians 2:8–9

"He who began a good work in you will carry it on to completion until the day of Christ Jesus." Philippians 1:6

God started the work. God will finish the work. Our part is to trust Him and walk with Him through the process in between.

In the Next Chapter...

We'll examine how salvation is presented differently for our spirit, soul, and body. This can be critical to understanding the process for sanctification, while still feeling secure in our salvation.

CHAPTER 2

SAVED, BEING SAVED, AND HELP ALONG THE WAY

When someone first believes in Jesus—when they place their trust in Him for salvation—something miraculous happens. At that moment, they are saved. But what exactly does that mean? Are they completely changed in every area of life? Or is something deeper going on beneath the surface?

The Bible paints a layered picture of salvation—one that involves our spirit, our soul, and, ultimately, even our body. Understanding these distinctions helps us not only make sense of our own growth, but also appreciate the gift of the Holy Spirit, who walks with us through every stage of that process.

Your Spirit: Saved and Sealed

At the moment of salvation, your spirit is made new. This is instantaneous. You go from death to life. You are reconciled to God. You are fully forgiven, fully accepted, and fully loved. Jesus tried to explain this to Nicodemus:

"Jesus answered, 'Very truly I tell you, no one can enter the kingdom of God unless they are born of water and the Spirit. Flesh gives birth to

flesh, but the Spirit gives birth to spirit. You should not be surprised at my saying, 'You must be born again.'" John 3:5-7

When we are born again, we are born of spirit. That is, God's Spirit comes into our spirit, bringing new life. Where else would the Holy Spirit reside?

"The Spirit himself testifies with our spirit that we are God's children."
Romans 8:16

"But whoever is united with the Lord is one with him in spirit." 1
Corinthians 6:17

The real you, your spirit, is joined to Christ. That part of you is completely saved, sealed, and secured.

"When you believed, you were marked in him with a seal, the promised Holy Spirit, who is a deposit guaranteeing our inheritance..." Ephesians 1:13–14

This is the foundation. Your salvation is not based on your performance, your progress, or your understanding. It's based on what Jesus did for you—and your spirit is now alive in Him.

Your Soul: Still Being Saved

But what about the rest of you? While your spirit is saved instantly, your soul—which includes your mind, will, and emotions—is in the process of being saved. This is where sanctification begins to unfold.

"Do not conform to the pattern of this world, but be transformed by the renewing of your mind." Romans 12:2

Your thoughts don't automatically change the moment you believe. Your reactions, your habits, your emotional wounds—those things don't disappear overnight. Instead, they begin to be renewed, re-shaped, and healed as you walk with Jesus. This is why James could write to believers and say:

"Therefore, get rid of all moral filth and the evil that is so prevalent and humbly accept the word planted in you, which can save you." James 1:21

Wait—"save you?" Weren't they already saved? Yes—but James is talking about the ongoing work of salvation in the soul. It's not a contradiction. It's a progression.

"Though you have not seen him, you love him; and even though you do not see him now, you believe in him and are filled with an inexpressible and glorious joy, for you are receiving the end result of your faith, the salvation of your souls." 1 Peter 1:8-9

Paul speaks to the Philippians about this process:

"But whatever were gains to me I now consider loss for the sake of Christ. What is more, I consider everything a loss because of the surpassing worth of knowing Christ Jesus my Lord, for whose sake I have lost all things. I consider them garbage, that I may gain Christ and be found in him, not having a righteousness of my own that comes from the law, but that which is through faith in Christ—the righteousness that comes from God on the basis of faith. I want to know Christ—yes, to know the power of his resurrection and participation in his sufferings, becoming like him in his death, and so, somehow, attaining to the resurrection from the dead. Not that I have already obtained all this, or have already arrived at my goal, but I press on to take hold of that for which Christ Jesus took hold of me. Brothers and sisters, I do not consider myself yet to have taken hold of it. But one thing I do: Forgetting what is behind and straining toward what is ahead, I press on toward the goal

to win the prize for which God has called me heavenward in Christ Jesus." Philippians 3:7-14

"Only let us live up to what we have already attained." Philippians 3:16

Your Body: Will Be Saved

The final stage of salvation will happen in the future, when Jesus returns and our bodies are made new. This is our great hope:

"But our citizenship is in heaven. And we eagerly await a Savior from there, the Lord Jesus Christ, who, by the power that enables him to bring everything under his control, will transform our lowly bodies so that they will be like his glorious body." Philippians 3:20-21

"...we ourselves, who have the firstfruits of the Spirit, groan inwardly as we wait eagerly for our adoption to sonship, the redemption of our bodies." Romans 8:23

In that moment, everything will be made whole. No more pain, no more sin, no more decay. But until then, we live in the in-between. Our spirits are saved. Our souls are being saved. Our bodies will be saved.

The Holy Spirit: Help for the Journey

So where does the Holy Spirit fit into all of this? The Holy Spirit lives in your spirit and He begins the work of transforming your soul. He is the one who teaches, convicts, comforts, strengthens, and leads.

"But the Advocate, the Holy Spirit, whom the Father will send in my name, will teach you all things and will remind you of everything I have said to you." John 14:26

"In the same way, the Spirit helps us in our weakness." Romans 8:26

You don't have to try harder to change yourself. That's not sanctification. Sanctification is letting the Holy Spirit lead the process. It's yielding your thoughts, emotions, and decisions to Him, moment by moment. He doesn't just point out what needs to change; He gives you the power to change it.

"...if by the Spirit you put to death the misdeeds of the body, you will live." Romans 8:13

The Spirit doesn't leave you to figure it out alone. He walks with you, works in you, and leads you deeper into the life of Christ. And as He does, your soul begins to look more and more like your spirit—alive, free, and whole. We'll discuss this in more detail in Chapter 4.

The Journey of Wholeness

Salvation is both an event and a journey.

- Your spirit is saved instantly.

- Your soul is being saved daily.

- Your body will be saved eventually.

- The Holy Spirit is with you through it all.

Understanding this helps you have grace for your own growth. It helps you recognize that transformation isn't proof that you're saved—it's the ongoing result of already being saved. It's not a test to pass, but a relationship to walk in.

So don't be discouraged if your emotions still flare up. Don't panic when old habits take time to break. Don't give up when your thoughts still need renewing. The Holy Spirit is at work in you. He hasn't left. He isn't frustrated. He's helping you, lovingly and patiently, to bring every part of you into the freedom Jesus already purchased.

"May God himself, the God of peace, sanctify you through and through. May your whole spirit, soul and body be kept blameless at the coming of our Lord Jesus Christ." 1 Thessalonians 5:23

You are saved. You are being saved. And you will be saved. And through it all, the Spirit is with you.

In the Next Chapter...

We'll examine how God views your completed sanctification, even as you're still in the process, and why that eternal perspective matters for how you live today. For now, be encouraged: if you're in Christ, you're a new creation, even if you're still learning how to live like one.

Chapter 3

God Sees the End from the Beginning

If you've ever looked in the mirror and felt disappointed with the person staring back at you, you're also not alone. It's one thing to know God loves you, but it can be hard to believe He sees you as holy, blameless, and complete when you feel so far from it. But what if I told you that God isn't surprised by your flaws? That He already sees the finished version of you and He loves you entirely, even now?

Let's start with a truth that anchors everything:

"I make known the end from the beginning, from ancient times, what is still to come. I say, 'My purpose will stand, and I will do all that I please.'" Isaiah 46:10

God is not like us. He doesn't move through time second by second. He exists outside of time and sees all of it at once. While we're caught in today's struggle, He sees our whole story, including how it ends.

When He saved you, He saw the entire arc of your life. He knew the moments you would fall short. He knew the detours you'd take. And He chose you anyway. That's what grace looks like from eternity.

The Eternal Lens of Love

To understand sanctification rightly, we must begin to see ourselves not just through the lens of time, but through the lens of eternity. When God looks at you, He sees the righteousness of Christ covering you. Not because you've earned it, but because Jesus gave it to you.

"God made him who had no sin to be sin for us, so that in him we might become the righteousness of God." 2 Corinthians 5:21

In *Him*, you *become* righteous. Not on your own. Not by trying harder. This righteousness is a gift, rooted in God's eternal plan for redemption—a plan He formed before you were born.

Paul makes this clear in his letter to the Ephesians:

"For he chose us in him before the creation of the world to be holy and blameless in his sight. In love he predestined us for adoption to sonship through Jesus Christ, in accordance with his pleasure and will–to the praise of his glorious grace, which he has freely given us in the One he loves." Ephesians 1:4–6

Before the creation of the world, God chose you. That means He wasn't caught off guard when you failed. He didn't choose you because you'd be flawless. He chose you in love, knowing that He would sanctify you step by step.

Already and Not Yet

There's a beautiful theological tension at work in Scripture called the "already and not yet." It means that some things are already true in God's eyes, even if we don't fully experience them yet. Here's how Paul describes it:

"But you were washed, you were sanctified, you were justified in the name of the Lord Jesus Christ and by the Spirit of our God." 1 Corinthians 6:11b

Sanctified—past tense. Done. Finished. But then in 1 Thessalonians, Paul writes:

"May God himself, the God of peace, sanctify you through and through. May your whole spirit, soul and body be kept blameless at the coming of our Lord Jesus Christ." 1 Thessalonians 5:23

Sanctify—present and future. Ongoing.

Both are true. This is the mystery and wonder of life in Christ. You are fully sanctified in the eyes of God because of Jesus. And you are being sanctified daily by the work of the Holy Spirit. The new creation is here, and it is still being formed.

We Live in Time, God Works in Eternity

Our frustration often comes from wanting eternal results in a temporal timeline. We want overnight change, instant freedom, and dramatic transformation. But God is a gardener, not a magician. He plants seeds, He prunes, He waters, and He waits.

Jesus described the kingdom of God in the same way:

"This is what the kingdom of God is like. A man scatters seed on the ground. Night and day, whether he sleeps or gets up, the seed sprouts and grows, though he does not know how. All by itself the soil produces grain—first the stalk, then the head, then the full kernel in the head. As soon as the grain is ripe, he puts the sickle to it, because the harvest has come." Mark 4:26–29

Growth happens in stages. It's not all visible at once, and it doesn't always make sense. But God is always working, even when we don't see the fruit yet.

The Danger of Temporal Thinking

When we judge our worth based on today's struggle, we risk believing lies. We tell ourselves:

- *I'm not really changing.*

- *God must be disappointed with me.*

- *I'll never get free from this habit.*

- *Other Christians seem to have it all together—what's wrong with me?*

However, these thoughts are rooted in a narrow and incomplete view of ourselves. God's perspective is wider, deeper, and eternal. He sees the full timeline of your sanctification, and He's not panicked about your pace. Instead, He invites you to trust His process.

What God Says About You

Let's take a moment to anchor our hearts in what God has already declared true about you, if you are in Christ. These verses are not future hopes; they are present realities in heaven, even if you're still learning to walk in them on earth:

"Therefore, there is now no condemnation for those who are in Christ Jesus, because through Christ Jesus the law of the Spirit who gives life has set you free from the law of sin and death." Romans 8:1–2

"You are all children of God through faith in Christ Jesus." Galatians 3:26

"You also were included in Christ when you heard the message of truth, the gospel of your salvation. When you believed, you were marked in him with a seal, the promised Holy Spirit, who is a deposit guaranteeing our inheritance until the redemption of those who are God's possession—to the praise of his glory." Ephesians 1:13–14

"For we are God's handiwork, created in Christ Jesus to do good works, which God prepared in advance for us to do." Ephesians 2:10

You are forgiven. Chosen. Loved. Redeemed. Indwelled by the Spirit. Marked for eternity. And none of that changes just because you're still being shaped.

Letting His View Shape Ours

If God sees you through the lens of eternity, perhaps you can start to offer yourself the same grace. Maybe the next time you stumble, instead of condemning yourself, you can pause and say:

"This isn't who I'm becoming. This isn't how God sees me. And this moment doesn't define me."

You are becoming someone glorious, because God is the One forming you. His fingerprints are all over your story.

"Yet you, Lord, are our Father. We are the clay, you are the potter; we are all the work of your hand." Isaiah 64:8

And He finishes what He starts.

"Being confident of this, that he who began a good work in you will carry it on to completion until the day of Christ Jesus." Philippians 1:6

In the Next Chapter...

We'll explore the central role of the Holy Spirit in sanctification and how to stop striving in the flesh and start walking in the Spirit's power. The transformation you long for is possible, but it doesn't come by human effort. It comes from God's presence living in you.

PART II:

THE PROCESS OF BECOMING

At one point in my life, I found myself at a revival meeting in Colorado Springs at a church I did not normally attend. The church was advertising that they were bringing the Toronto Blessing to our city. The Toronto Blessing revival was particularly known for its supernatural laughter and joy, among other notable characteristics. I was curious to learn more about it. Early in the service, a woman was asking for prayer for her husband who was on his deathbed with some sickness. She was in tears as she shared the circumstances. While she was sharing, some people a few rows in front of her started laughing. This seemed like a very odd and rude time to laugh, but the speaker didn't say anything. He just waited and little by little other people began laughing. As I looked around, I could tell other people were visibly nervous and confused. At this point, the leader started to speak about God pouring out His joy upon us, completely disregarding the earlier prayer request. He even went so far as to suggest that those of us who were not laughing were resisting—or even rejecting—the move of the Holy Spirit.

By this point, my wife and my mother, who had joined me, both wanted to leave. But I asked them to wait. I was praying the entire time, asking God to give me understanding of what was happening. Then, I had a very clear vision. It was only the second of three visions

I've had in my lifetime. I was standing in what looked like a Victorian painting of a lovely park, with big trees and a river flowing through the middle. I saw handsome men in suits with beautiful women in Victorian dresses, accompanied by parasol umbrellas, talking under the trees or sitting on blankets in the grass. There were others sitting on the bank of the river, with their pant legs or dresses rolled up, dangling their feet in the water. Then I saw some people in swimsuits wading knee-deep, even waist-deep. At last, I saw people fully immersed, swimming and playing in the water. Recognizing this all referred to our willingness to go deep in God, I said, *"Holy Spirit, that's where I am supposed to be, fully immersed and swimming in the living water, right?"* Then I heard Him gently respond, *"Look closer!"* As I looked again in the river, I saw human shapes that completely blended with the water and flowed with the current. There was nothing to distinguish them other than a barely visible human form, like a shadow. Then the Holy Spirit spoke again, saying, *"This is what I want from you, to flow with Me and be one with Me. The people in this room around you are like the people swimming. They are aware of me and my gifts, but they are using them as they please. They are not flowing with Me."* After that, we left the service and the leader made some negative comments about us as we walked out the door. To this day, the Holy Spirit reminds me of that vision many years ago as He teaches me about the process of becoming more like Him.

CHAPTER 4

THE POWER OF THE HOLY SPIRIT

If sanctification is a process, which it is, then the next question we must ask is, "*Who does the work?*" If we're not made instantly perfect at salvation, does that mean it's up to us to make ourselves holy? The short answer—no. The Christian life isn't about trying harder. It's about learning how to depend more fully on the presence of God, specifically the presence of the Holy Spirit living within us.

Many Christians believe in the Holy Spirit, but few live in daily dependence on Him. For years, I tried to be transformed by good intentions, discipline, and biblical knowledge. Those are all helpful things, but they are not the power source for sanctification. Only the Holy Spirit can truly change us from the inside out. As I shared in the "Introduction," I realized I couldn't even *love* God without His help.

The Promise of the Helper

Before Jesus went to the cross, He comforted His disciples with a remarkable promise:

"And I will ask the Father, and he will give you another advocate to help you and be with you forever—the Spirit of truth. The world cannot

accept him, because it neither sees him nor knows him. But you know him, for he lives with you and will be in you." John 14:16–17

Jesus was preparing them for life after His ascension. He wasn't leaving them to figure things out on their own. He was sending the Holy Spirit, the Advocate, the Comforter, the Spirit of Truth. And notice this: *"He will be in you."* This wasn't just about external guidance. The Holy Spirit would dwell within them, and within us.

Paul writes it this way:

"Do you not know that your bodies are temples of the Holy Spirit, who is in you, whom you have received from God? You are not your own; you were bought at a price. Therefore honor God with your bodies." 1 Corinthians 6:19–20

The same Spirit who hovered over the waters in Genesis now lives in you. The same Spirit who raised Jesus from the dead now empowers your daily life.

"And if the Spirit of him who raised Jesus from the dead is living in you, he who raised Christ from the dead will also give life to your mortal bodies because of his Spirit who lives in you." Romans 8:11

That's not poetry. That's power. And it's available to you right now.

Not by Might, Not by Power

The prophet Zechariah heard these words from the Lord while facing an impossible task:

"'Not by might nor by power, but by my Spirit,' says the Lord Almighty." Zechariah 4:6

That same truth applies to sanctification. You won't overcome sin by sheer determination. You won't change your mindset by gritting your teeth. You won't bear fruit by trying harder to be patient, loving, joyful, or kind. You'll bear fruit when you stay connected to the Source.

Jesus explained it this way:

"I am the vine; you are the branches. If you remain in me and I in you, you will bear much fruit; apart from me you can do nothing." John 15:5

The fruit of the Spirit is not something we manufacture. It's something we *bear*—the natural result of remaining in Christ and yielding to His Spirit.

Paul says:

"But the fruit of the Spirit is love, joy, peace, forbearance, kindness, goodness, faithfulness, gentleness and self-control. Against such things there is no law." Galatians 5:22–23

Notice that Paul doesn't call them the *fruits* of the Spirit. It's not plural. It's singular. These qualities are one unified result of the Spirit's work in a surrendered life. If you lack joy, peace or self-control, don't condemn yourself. That's not a signal to work harder. It's an invitation to draw nearer, to stay connected to the Vine.

Walking by the Spirit

One of the most practical teachings Paul offers on sanctification is found in Galatians:

"So I say, walk by the Spirit, and you will not gratify the desires of the flesh. For the flesh desires what is contrary to the Spirit, and the Spirit

what is contrary to the flesh. They are in conflict with each other, so that you are not to do whatever you want. But if you are led by the Spirit, you are not under the law." Galatians 5:16–18

"Walk by the Spirit." That's the key. Walking is not a frantic sprint. It's a daily, moment-by-moment awareness of the Spirit's presence and promptings. It's listening. Yielding. Obeying. Trusting. Sometimes it's failing, but quickly returning to dependence.

Paul goes on to contrast the works of the flesh with the fruit of the Spirit. However, what I want to highlight is that the word 'walk' implies a process. It implies movement. It implies progress, not perfection. You're not expected to teleport into holiness. You are called to walk with the Spirit who leads you there.

The Spirit Is Not Passive

Sometimes we imagine the Holy Spirit as a quiet force or a vague inner nudge. But Scripture describes Him as powerful, active, and deeply involved in our growth:

"Now the Lord is the Spirit, and where the Spirit of the Lord is, there is freedom. And we all, who with unveiled faces contemplate the Lord's glory, are being transformed into his image with ever-increasing glory, which comes from the Lord, who is the Spirit." 2 Corinthians 3:17–18

He is actively transforming us. We don't have to beg Him to do it. We have to surrender to Him, allowing Him to do it. Freedom doesn't come from trying to be free. It comes from the presence of the Lord. And transformation isn't a result of better effort. It's a result of beholding Him. As you spend time with God—reading His Word, sitting in silence, praying, worshiping—something happens that you can't manufacture: your desires change. Your thinking shifts. Your heart softens. That's the Spirit at work.

From Performance to Presence

For years, I tried to grow by performing better. I thought the more I controlled my thoughts, the more I resisted temptation, the more I looked like a mature Christian, then the holier I would become. I also read Scripture, prayed, and fasted; but I still trusted more in my effort than in His grace. After fifty years, I realized I was still trying to earn His love rather than just living in it. I knew in my head that I couldn't earn His love, yet in my heart and actions I was consumed with trying to. I needed the Holy Spirit to reveal my true motives to me.

Performance led to cycles of burnout, shame, and hiding. It wasn't until I learned to live in the presence of the Holy Spirit—to speak honestly with Him, to listen for His voice, to welcome His conviction without fear—that real change began to take root. When the Spirit convicts, it leads to healing, not hiding. When the Spirit leads, He also gives strength to follow. And when the Spirit empowers, the impossible becomes possible.

"You, however, are not in the realm of the flesh but are in the realm of the Spirit, if indeed the Spirit of God lives in you. And if anyone does not have the Spirit of Christ, they do not belong to Christ. But if Christ is in you, then even though your body is subject to death because of sin, the Spirit gives life because of righteousness." Romans 8:9–10

This isn't a theory. It's your inheritance. You don't need to earn the Holy Spirit's help. You simply need to receive it.

In the Next Chapter...

We'll look at what it means to die daily—to surrender our desires, ideas, and strength so that the life of Christ can be formed in us.

Sanctification is not just about learning to walk in the Spirit, but about choosing daily to lay down our flesh. With that surrender, we find something better than control; we find freedom.

CHAPTER 5

DAILY DYING, DAILY RISING

One of the most paradoxical truths of the Christian life is this: real life begins when we die. That's not just poetic language. It's the very framework Jesus gave us for following Him:

"Whoever wants to be my disciple must deny themselves and take up their cross daily and follow me. For whoever wants to save their life will lose it, but whoever loses their life for me will save it." Luke 9:23–24

The cross wasn't a metaphor in Jesus' day. It was an instrument of death. And Jesus told His followers plainly: if you want to truly live, you must first die. Not physically. Spiritually.

You die to your old self. Your pride. Your agenda. Your will. Your way. The Greek word "psuchē," used above in Luke 9:23, was understood to encompass the mind, will, and emotions. And here's the challenging part—it's not a one-time event. Jesus said, *"Take up your cross daily."* Sanctification is a daily surrender. A daily death. And through that death, God brings resurrection life.

What Does It Mean to Die Daily?

When Paul wrote to the Corinthian church, he didn't sugarcoat the cost of following Jesus. He said:

"I face death every day—yes, just as surely as I boast about you in Christ Jesus our Lord." 1 Corinthians 15:31

This wasn't just about physical danger. Paul was describing the spiritual discipline of dying to himself daily—laying down his ego, his comfort, and his rights to follow Christ.

In another letter, he puts it more bluntly:

"I have been crucified with Christ and I no longer live, but Christ lives in me. The life I now live in the body, I live by faith in the Son of God, who loved me and gave himself for me." Galatians 2:20

This is the heart of sanctification: Christ living in us. But in order for that to happen, something has to get out of the way. And that something is us—our flesh, our self-life, our old way of thinking.

Paul writes in Romans:

"We were therefore buried with him through baptism into death in order that, just as Christ was raised from the dead through the glory of the Father, we too may live a new life." Romans 6:4

You were buried with Christ. But are you living like someone who died? Most of us don't like the idea of surrender. It feels like weakness. Like giving up. But, in the kingdom of God, surrender is the pathway to strength.

"For when I am weak, then I am strong." 2 Corinthians 12:10b

"Father, if you are willing, take this cup from me; yet not my will, but yours be done." Luke 22:42

Daily dying is not self-hatred. It's not self-neglect. It's not giving up on becoming whole. It's giving up on doing it your way. It's saying, *"God, I trust Your Spirit to lead me better than I can lead myself."*

The War Within

Paul described the internal conflict we all feel:

"Those who live according to the flesh have their minds set on what the flesh desires; but those who live in accordance with the Spirit have their minds set on what the Spirit desires. The mind governed by the flesh is death, but the mind governed by the Spirit is life and peace. The mind governed by the flesh is hostile to God; it does not submit to God's law, nor can it do so. Those who are in the realm of the flesh cannot please God." Romans 8:5–8

That's sobering. But Paul isn't saying this to shame us. He's saying it to set us free. If we know the flesh leads to death, then we can make an intentional choice to live by the Spirit. But here's the key: that choice must be made again and again. Every day. Sometimes every hour. We die daily. And each time we do, more of Christ's life rises in us.

The Practical Side of Surrender

So what does daily dying look like in everyday life?

It might look like...

- Choosing to forgive someone who doesn't deserve it, because Jesus forgave you.

- Holding your tongue in an argument, even when you're right.

- Confessing a hidden sin to a trusted friend or mentor, instead of continuing in secrecy.

- Saying no to something you want because you sense the

Spirit saying it's not best for you.

- Admitting your weakness and asking God for help—again.

- Choosing to speak kindly to, and about, someone who has slandered you.

None of those things are glamorous. But they are holy. They are the small, unseen acts of surrender that God uses to sanctify you.

"Therefore, I urge you, brothers and sisters, in view of God's mercy, to offer your bodies as a living sacrifice, holy and pleasing to God—this is your true and proper worship. Do not conform to the pattern of this world, but be transformed by the renewing of your mind. Then you will be able to test and approve what God's will is—his good, pleasing and perfect will." Romans 12:1–2

Who offers your body as a living sacrifice? You do – your spirit. How do you offer it? You present your body as a living sacrifice by renewing your mind, surrendering your mind to be controlled by the Spirit, instead of by your flesh. A living sacrifice. Renewed mind. Transformed life. But first, surrender.

Death Brings Life

In the natural world, death feels final. But in God's economy, death is never the end. It's the beginning.

Jesus said:

"Very truly I tell you, unless a kernel of wheat falls to the ground and dies, it remains only a single seed. But if it dies, it produces many seeds." John 12:24

When we die to self, we make room for something greater to grow. Life. Fruit. Multiplication. And that's exactly what sanctification is: dying to our old nature so the new life of Christ can bear fruit through us.

Resurrection Power for Every Day

The good news is that you're not asked to die daily in your own strength. The same power that raised Jesus from the dead lives in you. We saw this in the last chapter, but it bears repeating here:

"And if the Spirit of him who raised Jesus from the dead is living in you, he who raised Christ from the dead will also give life to your mortal bodies because of his Spirit who lives in you." Romans 8:11

This means that you don't have to fear surrender. The Holy Spirit meets you in your weakness. He breathes resurrection life into places you thought were long dead—desires, emotions, relationships, dreams. Think of the Valley of Dry Bones in Ezekiel 37:1-14, where God asks Ezekiel to prophesy over dry bones and they come to life. In the end, read what God says:

"Then he said to me: 'Son of man, these bones are the people of Israel. They say, 'Our bones are dried up and our hope is gone; we are cut off.' Therefore prophesy and say to them: 'This is what the Sovereign Lord says: My people, I am going to open your graves and bring you up from them; I will bring you back to the land of Israel. Then you, my people, will know that I am the Lord, when I open your graves and bring you up from them. I will put my Spirit in you and you will live, and I will settle you in your own land. Then you will know that I the Lord have spoken, and I have done it,' declares the Lord." Ezekiel 37:11-14

He begins by talking about their hopes and dreams that have died and then concludes by saying, "I will put my Spirit in you and you will live." Daily dying is not just the path to sanctification. It's the doorway to joy. It's how you get free.

In the Next Chapter...

We'll explore the concept of renewing the mind and how your thought life plays a crucial role in the sanctification process. Scripture tells us to be transformed by the renewing of our minds, so how exactly does that happen? And how do we stop agreeing with old lies and start walking in truth? Get ready to go deeper.

CHAPTER 6

RENEWING THE MIND

Looking back in my journal after initially writing this chapter, I came across an entry from almost three years ago. I had an unusual and vivid dream, so I had written it down. In the dream, my wife and I were in a random house and, as I looked up at the ceiling, I saw a hole. It was about the size of a bowling ball and it went from the ceiling right through to the roof. On the ceiling side, there was a spider web with a big spider. On the roof side there were layers of plastic and paper with something wrapped inside. I realized that inside the plastic and paper was a developing baby fetus. I quickly went out to a patio, found a ladder, and climbed up on the roof. I was trying to release the baby from the layers of plastic and paper so that I could get it away from the giant spider. I became almost frantic. It seemed that for every layer I tore away, there was yet another layer below. But then the baby began moving towards me, pushing against the final layer of plastic until its head suddenly burst through. I was shocked to find not a fetus, but a fully formed baby in my arms. I could not wait to show my wife.

Just a few weeks prior to this dream, I had written in my journal that I had arrived at a point with only two options: either God's Word wasn't true or I didn't truly believe the things I claimed to believe—because I clearly wasn't walking in the fullness of the promises I read in His Word. At the time of the dream, I thought it might be revealing the birthing of some new ministry we would get involved in or something external. As I reread this dream now, I realize it was about me becoming completely "born again." For so many years, I was a fetus. I had the DNA of Christ and His Word in me, but I was struggling to really experience the fruit of the Holy Spirit in my life. The spider, web, and layers of garbage that kept me from growing are the things that, in these last few years, God has been stripping away from me: a spirit of rejection, a religious spirit and judgemental mindset, lack of understanding of the Father's heart, pride, and so many other things. I truly became more desperate in these last few years to be free of those hindrances, as He revealed them to me one by one, and to know the fullness of His life in me. Now, as I am writing this, I feel more like that fully formed baby. I am being held joyfully by the Father and finally experiencing more of the promised fruit of the Spirit in my life. Being born again requires a new way of thinking. If you want to change your life, you have to change the way you think. That's not just motivational talk, it is biblical truth. The Apostle Paul wrote these famous words to the believers in Rome:

"Therefore, I urge you, brothers and sisters, in view of God's mercy, to offer your bodies as a living sacrifice, holy and pleasing to God—this is your true and proper worship. Do not conform to the pattern of this world, but be transformed by the renewing of your mind. Then you will be able to test and approve what God's will is—his good, pleasing and perfect will." Romans 12:1–2

Let's break this down.

Transformation Starts in the Mind

Notice Paul doesn't say, *"Be transformed by trying harder,"* or *"Be transformed by feeling bad about your sin."* He says, *"Be transformed by the renewing of your mind."*

In other words, what you believe matters. What you dwell on shapes you. What you think about becomes the filter through which you see the world and yourself. Many of us attempt to change our behavior without addressing the underlying beliefs. But behavior is the fruit. Belief is the root.

To make this more clear, here are a few everyday examples that show how behavior often grows out of deeper, hidden beliefs and how Scripture can help us replace those beliefs with truth:

Example 1: People-Pleasing

Behavior: Constantly saying "yes" to others, even when you're overwhelmed.

Root Belief: "If I say no, they won't like me or I'll be rejected." (Fear of rejection)

People-pleasing behavior is rooted in a belief that your worth is tied to others' approval.

Scriptural Response:

"Am I now trying to win the approval of human beings, or of God? ... If I were still trying to please people, I would not be a servant of Christ." Galatians 1:10

"The Lord is with me; I will not be afraid. What can mere mortals do to me?" Psalm 118:6

"Accept one another, then, just as Christ accepted you, in order to bring praise to God." Romans 15:7

Affirmation of Truth:

"I am fully accepted by God and I no longer live for the approval of people. I am not afraid of rejection, because the Lord is with me. I serve Christ, not human opinion, and His acceptance is enough for me."

Example 2: Emotional Eating

Behavior: Turning to food for comfort or stress relief.

Root Belief: "This is the only thing that gives me peace or helps me cope." (Fear of losing control)

Overeating is often rooted in the belief that food is the safest or most reliable source of comfort, rather than God. It helps us feel in control when everything around us is out of control.

Scriptural Response:

"Taste and see that the Lord is good; blessed is the one who takes refuge in him." Psalm 34:8

"Cast all your anxiety on him because he cares for you." 1 Peter 5:7

"Jesus answered, 'It is written: 'Man shall not live on bread alone, but on every word that comes from the mouth of God.''" Matthew 4:4

Affirmation of Truth:

"I find my true comfort and peace in the presence of God. He cares for me and I cast all my anxiety on Him. His Word nourishes me more deeply than food ever could, and I take refuge in His goodness."

Example 3: Gossip

Behavior: Talking about others behind their backs.

Root Belief: "If I point out their flaws, I'll feel better about myself." (Fear of rejection and loneliness)

Gossip can be rooted in insecurity and a belief that your value comes from comparison.

Scriptural Response:

"Do not let any unwholesome talk come out of your mouths, but only what is helpful for building others up..." Ephesians 4:29

"In humility, value others above yourselves." Philippians 2:3

"Dear friends, since God so loved us, we also ought to love one another ...We love because he first loved us." 1 John 4:11,19

Affirmation of Truth:

"I speak words that build others up, not tear them down. I humbly choose to value other people, knowing my worth is secure in God's love. Because He loves me, I choose to love others with my words and actions."

Example 4: Perfectionism at Work

Behavior: Obsessively checking your work and never feeling it's good enough.

Root Belief: "If I make a mistake, I'll be exposed as a failure or fraud." (Fear of failure)

Perfectionism is often rooted in fear and a belief that your identity is based on performance.

Scriptural Response:

"My grace is sufficient for you, for my power is made perfect in weakness." 2 Corinthians 12:9

"There is now no condemnation for those who are in Christ Jesus." Romans 8:1

"But God demonstrates his own love for us in this: While we were still sinners, Christ died for us." Romans 5:8

Affirmation of Truth:

"I am not defined by my performance. God's grace is enough for me and His power shines through my weakness. I am fully loved, fully accepted, and free from condemnation because of Christ."

Example 5: Social Media Obsession

Behavior: Constantly checking likes, comments, and posting curated content.

Root Belief: "I need to prove I'm valuable or interesting to others." (Fear of not having value)

The behavior is fruit; the root is a belief that your worth must be validated externally.

Scriptural Response:

"You are all children of God through faith in Christ Jesus." Galatians 3:26

"The LORD does not look at the things people look at... the LORD looks at the heart." 1 Samuel 16:7

"But you are a chosen people, a royal priesthood, a holy nation, God's special possession, that you may declare the praises of him who called you out of darkness into his wonderful light. Once you were not a people, but now you are the people of God; once you had not received mercy, but now you have received mercy." 1 Peter 2:9-10

Affirmation of Truth:

"I don't need the world's approval to know that I matter. I am God's child, chosen and deeply loved. My value comes from who I am in Christ, not from how others respond to me."

Example 6: Hiding Spiritual Struggles

Behavior: Acting like everything is "fine" at church and avoiding vulnerability.

Root Belief: "If I'm honest, people will think I'm weak or not spiritual enough." (Fear of shame)

This behavior is rooted in shame and a belief that you must maintain a certain image to be accepted.

Scriptural Response:

"Therefore confess your sins to each other and pray for each other so that you may be healed." James 5:16

"But he said to me, 'My grace is sufficient for you, for my power is made perfect in weakness.'" 2 Corinthians 12:9

"Therefore, since we are surrounded by such a great cloud of witnesses, let us throw off everything that hinders and the sin that so easily entan-

gles. And let us run with perseverance the race marked out for us, fixing our eyes on Jesus, the pioneer and perfecter of faith. For the joy set before him he endured the cross, scorning its shame, and sat down at the right hand of the throne of God. Consider him who endured such opposition from sinners, so that you will not grow weary and lose heart." Hebrews 12:1-3

Affirmation of Truth:

"I don't have to hide my struggles to be accepted. God's power is made perfect in my weakness, and healing comes when I walk in honesty. Jesus took my shame on the cross. I fix my eyes on Jesus—not perfection—and I am not alone. "

_____

Until your thoughts change, your life won't. Notice that the common denominator for most of the wrong thoughts we have is fear. Yet the Bible says:

"There is no fear in love. But perfect love drives out fear, because fear has to do with punishment. The one who fears is not made perfect in love." 1 John 4:18

The only way to change these thought patterns is to know His love for us, not just with Scripture in our head, but with experience in our hearts. We need to meditate on these Scriptures about our identity in Christ Jesus until we experientially know them, just as Adam "knew" Eve and they conceived a child (Gen. 4:1 KJV). We need to know God's love in a way that the Holy Spirit conceives new life and new thinking in us.

The Pattern of the World vs. the Pattern of the Kingdom

Paul also says, *"Do not conform to the pattern of this world…"* Romans *12:2.* This world has a pattern—a way of thinking, living, and reacting. It's rooted in pride, self-protection, comparison, entitlement, fear, and striving. Some of you are already identifying with these patterns as you read them. If you don't intentionally renew your mind, you will unintentionally conform to the world's pattern. But the kingdom of God has a different pattern. It's rooted in love, humility, trust, grace, surrender, and truth. Jesus lived and taught this pattern. The Sermon on the Mount is a beautiful and radical example:

"You have heard that it was said, 'Love your neighbor and hate your enemy.' But I tell you, love your enemies and pray for those who persecute you, that you may be children of your Father in heaven. He causes his sun to rise on the evil and the good, and sends rain on the righteous and the unrighteous." Matthew 5:43–45

Loving enemies? Blessing those who curse you? That's not worldly thinking. That's kingdom thinking. And it takes a renewed mind to live that way.

Taking Every Thought Captive

In another letter, Paul describes how spiritual transformation involves demolishing lies and replacing them with truth:

"The weapons we fight with are not the weapons of the world. On the contrary, they have divine power to demolish strongholds. We demolish arguments and every pretension that sets itself up against the knowledge of God, and we take captive every thought to make it obedient to Christ." 2 Corinthians 10:4–5

Think of your mind like a battlefield. Not every thought you have is from God. Some thoughts come from your flesh, some from past wounds, and some from the enemy who wants to keep you bound. The call to "take captive every thought" means we examine our thoughts, compare them to God's truth, and reject what doesn't align.

You don't have to believe every thought that enters your mind. And you certainly don't have to be controlled by it. The problem is that the longer we meditate on an idea, the more true it becomes to us. Have you ever met a pathological liar and seen how they truly believe their lies? We are the same way. When we first get the impression that someone doesn't like or accept us and we begin to feel rejected, we can either begin to stew on that feeling, or we can immediately quote Scripture. We can remind ourselves that we are loved and accepted in Christ Jesus, and then shake off that rejection. With the love of the Father, we are able to love that person whether they love us or not, and it does not have to affect any of our other relationships. If we don't do this, but instead begin to focus on and meditate on the feeling of rejection, it grows into a stronghold of perceived truth. This will not only affect our relationship with that person, but it will also impact our relationships with others, including God.

Fighting the Enemy with the Sword of Scripture

"For the word of God is alive and active. Sharper than any double-edged sword, it penetrates even to dividing soul and spirit, joints and marrow; it judges the thoughts and attitudes of the heart." Hebrews 4:12

Another important note as we talk about the power of Scripture, God's written Word for us, is that Satan also uses Scripture. Read the story of Jesus' temptation in the wilderness in Matthew 4. After Jesus conquered the first temptation with the written Word and declared that we shall live by every Word that proceeds from the mouth of God, the enemy tries to trick Jesus by using the written Word of God too. It is not enough to have a Scripture for your circumstance, but you must have the "right" Scripture for your circumstance. This is a skill that you can develop as you mature as a believer and the Holy Spirit teaches you greater discernment. Moreover, as you spend time in intentional community with other believers, you can help each other to discern the appropriate Scripture for situations that may arise.

For example, my wife and I were on a bike ride with dear friends, one of whom is a dedicated cyclist. Luke had convinced the rest of us to ride up a steep mountain with him. On the way up, I was joking about the Scripture that says:

"Truly I tell you, if anyone says to this mountain, 'Go, throw yourself into the sea,' and does not doubt in their heart but believes that what they say will happen, it will be done for them." Mark 11:23

And I said to the mountain, "Be removed from us and be made flat." My wife quickly responded and said, "No, the correct word is:

'I can do all this through him who gives me strength' (Philippians 4:13)."

We then marveled at the idea of not just having a Word, but having the right Word at the right time in our lives. I was using Scripture in a presumptuous way, the same way that Satan was tempting Jesus to use Scripture in his second temptation in Matthew 4. My wife was using an appropriate Scripture for the circumstance we were facing.

This is a simple example, but it demonstrates the wisdom and power that God can bring forward when we are in fellowship with other Spirit-filled believers. One way to think of it is in the context of sparring for sword-fighting, where sword fighters will practice with one another to prepare themselves for the real battles. The Word of God is our sword. However, to learn to use it well, it is good to spar with our brothers and sisters in Christ so that we don't harm ourselves, but instead bring harm to the enemy. Through sparring, we can help each other find the right Word of God for the circumstances or trials we find ourselves in.

What You Believe About God Matters

At the root of many of our struggles is a distorted view of God.

- If you believe He's distant, you'll try to manage life on your own.

- If you believe He's angry, you'll live in fear and shame.

- If you believe He's passive, you'll feel unprotected and unseen.

However, the truth is that God is near. He's kind. He's powerful. And He's actively working in your life, even when you don't see it. Here's what Scripture says about who He really is:

"The Lord is compassionate and gracious, slow to anger, abounding in love." Psalm 103:8

"The Lord is close to the brokenhearted and saves those who are crushed in spirit." Psalm 34:18

"Every good and perfect gift is from above, coming down from the Father of the heavenly lights, who does not change like shifting shadows." James 1:17

Sometimes these distorted views come from the teaching we've received in church. Sometimes they come from the relationships around us; especially from our fathers, since God identifies Himself as the Father. If your father was distant, angry, or passive, you will likely think of God that way.

About a year and a half before writing this book, I was visiting my adult children in Colorado. Early one morning, I was sitting in a comfortable chair next to the gas fireplace in my son's and daughter's house, just starting a quiet time with the Lord, when suddenly the Holy Spirit spoke before I could. He said, *"You don't know how to relate to me as your Father because you've never had a good earthly father."* This happened every morning for the next four days, as He showed me how I had grown independent over the years. My parents divorced when I was three years old and my mom remarried about one year later. My biological dad moved to another state. After a few summer visits in the early years, my sisters and I didn't see him again until our high school graduations. He had his hands full with his new wife and seven children, so there was no close bonding for me. My stepdad was present growing up, but he was very temperamental and often negative. This made me reluctant to approach him with questions or problems. Therefore, I became a very independent self-learner. This same attitude had followed me into my Christian walk and 30 years of ministry. I didn't really trust God with my problems or decisions. I would pray about them, but then handle them on my own. I didn't know what it was supposed to look like to trust Him as my loving Father.

On the fifth day of this discussion with the Holy Spirit, it started differently. He said, *"Because you didn't have a good father, you haven't been a good father. You couldn't give to your children what you had never experienced."* This did not come as condemnation, but as a demonstration of God's love, showing me where I could have done better with my children. It was not to shame me for my past mistakes, but to give me the wisdom and knowledge I needed to do better now and in the future. Right away, I saw how I had passed on that very independent spirit to two of my three children and how it began interfering in our relationship with them as adults. My children never rebelled. They still followed the Lord, but our ties as a family seemed increasingly strained—as evidenced by increasingly short phone calls from Europe to America. Now I knew why. It took a couple of days to build up the courage, but then I asked my children to forgive me. They admitted to feeling some wounds over the years, as I was not emotionally present and supportive the way I should have been and had expected them to be independent like me; especially in their teen years, which had been the most difficult time for me growing up. They forgave me. Now our relationship is so much better and deeper, as is my relationship with God. I released my independence and returned to His Fatherly love, a love I had never known experientially until then. I now find it much easier to depend on God's strength and wisdom rather than my own, to trust Him in the things I don't understand, and to give more grace to others who aren't independent and able to figure things out on their own.

If you want to be sanctified, you must renew your mind with the truth of who God really is. When you see Him rightly, everything else starts to shift.

What You Believe About Yourself Matters

Renewing your mind also means confronting lies you believe about yourself. Lies like:

- *I'll never change.*

- *I'm too broken.*

- *God can't use someone like me.*

- *I have to earn God's love.*

- *I always mess things up.*

These thoughts are not harmless. They are strongholds. But the Word of God has the power to tear them down.

"Therefore, if anyone is in Christ, the new creation has come: The old has gone, the new is here!" 2 Corinthians 5:17

"There is now no condemnation for those who are in Christ Jesus." Romans 8:1

"You are all children of God through faith in Christ Jesus." Galatians 3:26

"The weapons we fight with are not the weapons of the world. On the contrary, they have divine power to demolish strongholds. We demolish arguments and every pretension that sets itself up against the knowledge of God, and we take captive every thought to make it obedient to Christ." 2 Corinthians 10:4-5

As you meditate on these truths, your mind begins to be renewed. And that renewal leads to real transformation. Notice, in reference to demolishing strongholds, Paul mentions explicitly arguments and thoughts. Don't let lies become strongholds; refute them quickly. If they have become strongholds, you are still given weapons with "divine power to demolish strongholds." You don't have to live in those lies anymore.

Practical Steps for Renewing Your Mind

So, how do you actually *do* this?

Here are a few simple but powerful steps:

1. **Read the Word daily** – Let Scripture shape your thoughts more than social media, news, or your own emotions. If you're thinking *I already do that,* I encourage you to use your phone usage settings to track how much time you spend on social media and the news in a day compared to your time in the Word. This is not for condemnation, but rather to be sure that we are accountable to the truth and not deceiving ourselves.

2. **Memorize key verses** – Arm yourself with truth for the moments when lies come knocking. Jesus answered Satan's temptations with Scripture; you must do the same. When you feel your identity as a child of God is challenged or God's goodness is challenged, quoting the truth of Scripture is the quickest and most effective way to silence the voice of lies. There are many Scriptures in this book that you could begin with. There is also a list of affirmations concerning your identity in Christ in the back of the book.

3. **Write down lies you believe** – And next to each one, write a corresponding Scripture that speaks the truth. If you need help finding the right Scriptures, ask a trusted friend or mentor for guidance. The journey of sanctification wasn't intended to be travelled alone.

4. **Speak truth out loud** – Your ears need to hear your mouth declare what God says. We discussed earlier how fear is often at the forefront of some wrong beliefs and thoughts. Fear is dealt with in the amygdala, the "fight or flight" portion of the brain. Scientists have now discovered that when we discuss our stress, it helps our brain shift the issue to the

prefrontal cortex, allowing us to reason and act rationally. Science is now catching up to what Jesus already knew: speak truth to the lies, problems, fears, and temptations around you. What seemed like a mountain because of fear-creating lies will then become a small bump in the road as you declare truth and are able to rationally compare the lie to the Truth of God's Word.

5. **Scripture Sparring** – Invite other trusted Believers into your personal battles. Allow them to hear the Scriptures you're using and to tell you what Scriptures they think may be more appropriate for your circumstances.

6. **Ask the Holy Spirit to reveal root beliefs** – Sometimes the thoughts we battle come from deeper, heart-level beliefs that need healing. I felt rejected from a very early age and carried that feeling into my relationships throughout my life. I was independent because I thought I could not depend on others to help me. That was my childhood experience after all. Let the Holy Spirit reveal your root beliefs and heal them, just as He has been doing for me.

This is not about becoming a Bible robot. It's about learning to think the way heaven thinks. That's what sanctification does—it brings heaven's truth to earth, starting in our own mind.

In the Next Chapter...

We'll look at how sanctification also involves putting on the new self and learning new patterns, practices, and habits that align with who God says we are. Transformation isn't just about what we stop doing—it's also about what we start doing by faith.

CHAPTER 7

PUTTING ON THE NEW SELF

Sanctification isn't just about what we leave behind. It's also about what we step into. You don't just take off the old clothes of sin, shame, and self-effort—you put on the wardrobe of your new identity in Christ. It's a conscious, daily decision to walk in who God says you are, not who you used to be.

The Apostle Paul makes this idea clear in Ephesians:

"You were taught, with regard to your former way of life, to put off your old self, which is being corrupted by its deceitful desires; to be made new in the attitude of your minds; and to put on the new self, created to be like God in true righteousness and holiness." Ephesians 4:22–24

This is a process. And it requires intention. Just as a person doesn't accidentally get dressed in the morning, we don't automatically put on the new self without thought or choice. Again, we see the mind is involved – "be made new in the attitude of your minds." But unlike physical clothing, this "new self" isn't something you put on to look better—it's the expression of your true identity in Christ.

The Old Self vs. the New Self

Paul often speaks in contrasts: death and life, flesh and spirit, old and new.

In Colossians, he expands the concept:

"Do not lie to each other, since you have taken off your old self with its practices and have put on the new self, which is being renewed in knowledge in the image of its Creator." Colossians 3:9–10

Notice the wording: *"taken off the old self with its practices."* The old self has *"practices,"* ways of thinking and acting that become habitual. In other words, sin doesn't just show up in behavior, it embeds itself in patterns.

When you come to Christ, those patterns don't disappear overnight. They must be unlearned and new patterns—new practices—must be learned in their place. This is where sanctification meets discipleship. Yes, the Spirit does change your desires, but He also invites you to practice new habits that align with those new desires.

Habits of the New Self

The new self also has practices—holy habits—that don't earn God's favor but flow from it.

Let's look again at Colossians, continuing a few verses later:

"Therefore, as God's chosen people, holy and dearly loved, clothe yourselves with compassion, kindness, humility, gentleness and patience. Bear with each other and forgive one another if any of you has a grievance against someone. Forgive as the Lord forgave you. And over

all these virtues put on love, which binds them all together in perfect unity." Colossians 3:12–14

That's the wardrobe of the sanctified life.

These virtues don't come naturally to our flesh, but they are the natural outgrowth of life in the Spirit. And, like any skill, they grow through practice.

Putting on the new self means choosing:

- Compassion over criticism

- Kindness over defensiveness

- Humility over pride

- Forgiveness over resentment

- Love over indifference

These aren't just lofty ideas—they're daily decisions.

Training, Not Trying

Many believers become stuck here. They know they should be loving, forgiving, and kind, but trying harder doesn't seem to work. That's because sanctification isn't about trying, it's about training. Paul uses that language deliberately:

"Have nothing to do with godless myths and old wives' tales; rather, train yourself to be godly. For physical training is of some value, but godliness has value for all things, holding promise for both the present life and the life to come." 1 Timothy 4:7–8

Training means you don't have to be perfect on day one. It means you show up, you repeat, you fail, you grow, and you keep going. Spiritual disciplines like prayer, fasting, Scripture meditation, silence, worship, and community accountability are all part of how we train to walk in the Spirit and put on the new self. You can't transform yourself, but you can participate in the process. You can show up for the training.

Identity Comes Before Behavior

One of the most freeing truths in Scripture is this: your identity in Christ comes before your behavior. Paul reminds the Colossians: *"As God's chosen people, holy and dearly loved..."* Before he gives a list of what to *"put on,"* he reminds them who they already are. You don't clothe yourself in good works to become holy, you do it because you are holy. You don't forgive to earn love, you forgive because you are already *"dearly loved."* This is the difference between religion and a relationship.

Religion says: *"Act holy so God will accept you."* The gospel says: *"God accepts you, so now you are free to walk in holiness."* Understanding this changes everything. It removes the pressure to perform and replaces it with the joy of responding to love.

"We love because he first loved us." 1 John 4:19

Sanctification is not a performance. It's a response.

When You Don't Feel New

There will be days when putting on the new self feels unnatural. There will be moments when anger feels more satisfying than patience, when fear screams louder than faith, when old patterns feel easier than new ones. That's okay.

Sanctification is not about pretending you're perfect. It's about returning—again and again—to the truth of who you are in Christ and choosing to align your actions with that truth, even when you don't feel it. Even when you fail and have to try again tomorrow. This is how we grow.

"And let us not grow weary in doing good, for at the proper time we will reap a harvest if we do not give up." Galatians 6:9

In the Next Chapter...

We'll discuss more about science and how epigenetics can help us understand the concept of sanctification. Often, what takes place in the physical realm parallels what is happening in the spiritual realm. God is a God of order and structure, and when we understand and follow His order, sanctification will follow.

CHAPTER 8

SANCTIFICATION AND SPIRITUAL EPIGENETICS

Science is catching up to what the Spirit has been doing all along. One fascinating area of study is epigenetics, which shows how our environment, experiences, and choices can literally influence how our genes are expressed. Through a process called methylation, certain parts of our DNA are either activated or silenced—not by altering the genes themselves, but by changing how they're read and used by the body.

This is a powerful image for spiritual growth and sanctification. Spiritually, we are born again with the "DNA" of Christ—His nature implanted in us. But the expression of that nature in our daily lives depends on our spiritual environment. Our thoughts, relationships, habits, and surroundings all affect how that spiritual DNA is either revealed or suppressed.

Jesus hinted at this dynamic in the Parable of the Sower:

"The seed falling on good soil refers to someone who hears the word and understands it. This is the one who produces a crop, yielding a hundred, sixty or thirty times what was sown." Matthew 13:23

The same seed is sown in all kinds of soil, but the outcome depends on the environment. Hard paths, rocky ground, and thorny distractions prevent the seed from maturing. But in good soil, the life hidden in the seed is fully expressed.

Your Environment Shapes Your Expression

Like methylation in our DNA, our spiritual growth is influenced by:

- The people we surround ourselves with

- What we listen to and watch

- The community and mentors we allow to speak into our lives

- How vulnerable and honest we're willing to be

James 5:16 reminds us of the power of vulnerability:

"Therefore confess your sins to each other and pray for each other so that you may be healed. The prayer of a righteous person is powerful and effective."

Healing and growth often come not just from private prayer, but from safe and honest relationships. When we bring our struggles to light in the context of a grace-filled community, our spiritual DNA finds the freedom to express itself fully.

Paul modeled this kind of spiritual mentorship with Timothy:

"To Timothy my true son in the faith: Grace, mercy and peace from God the Father and Christ Jesus our Lord." 1 Timothy 1:2

Paul didn't just teach Timothy, he fathered him in the faith. Sanctification was not just a personal process, but a relational one, lived out in the context of spiritual family.

The Influence of Media and Culture

Today, we are saturated with input. Music, podcasts, news, and social media—these are part of our daily environment. And just like diet affects the body's gene expression, what we feed on spiritually affects what is awakened or suppressed in our walk with Christ.

This is not about legalism. We are not trying to earn holiness. But when we truly love Jesus and want His life to be fully expressed in us, we begin to make intentional choices about our environment. We filter our input, not out of obligation, but out of love.

"'I have the right to do anything,' you say—but not everything is beneficial. 'I have the right to do anything'—but I will not be mastered by anything." 1 Corinthians 6:12

We choose better soil so that the seed can grow. We choose community, so we don't grow in isolation. We choose truth, so lies can't take root. We choose to dwell where the Spirit is moving, so that our spiritual DNA can be activated in its fullness.

Sanctification Is a Dance

God gave me an image that I'll never forget: sanctification is like a dance.

Jesus is the lead. Through the Holy Spirit, He guides every movement. We are the bride—the female partner in the dance—invited to follow. As long as our eyes are locked on His, the rhythm flows. The steps align. The beauty of the dance is undeniable. People watching are moved, not because we're skilled, but because they see the harmony between us and the Spirit.

But the moment we take our eyes off Him—glancing around at others, or down at our own feet—we stumble. We lose the rhythm. We throw off the grace of the moment. The key is not perfection, but focus. Not striving, but trusting. Sanctification flows when we stop leading and start following.

Let Jesus lead the dance. Let the Spirit set the rhythm. Choose the right environment. Plant yourself in good soil. Stay close to those who remind you of who you are and who let the life of Christ—the spiritual DNA within you—be fully expressed.

In the Next Chapter...

We'll take a deeper look at trust and rest—how sanctification grows not only through surrender and obedience, but also through learning to trust God's timing and rest in His work, not our own striving. Sometimes, the most spiritual thing you can do is to actually stop trying so hard.

CHAPTER 9

TRUSTING AND RESTING

In the harsh deserts of the American Southwest, tiny poppy seeds lie buried beneath the desert soil—often for many years—waiting. They don't sprout just because time has passed. They wait for the right conditions. Only when the soil has enough moisture to sustain life do they begin to grow, bursting into vibrant orange blossoms against the dry, barren landscape. These seeds teach us something profound: growth doesn't have to be forced. Like the desert poppy, we can trust that God knows when the conditions are right. Sanctification isn't about striving harder—it's about learning to rest in the One who controls the seasons. He knows when to water the soil of our hearts. Our job is to trust Him enough to wait.

Have you ever been prepared to dedicate a time to the Lord in worship, prayer, and reading, only to find yourself overwhelmed with sleepiness before you have hardly gotten started? What are the first thoughts that go through your head? If you are like I have been most of my life, the thoughts are of guilt and shame—neither of which comes from the Holy Spirit. Even when Jesus' disciples slept during His agonizing prayer in Gethsemane, He didn't condemn or shame them. Why do we think He would do that to us? What if it is God calling us into that rest or sleep, because He knows we need it? What if He knows we will enter His presence more easily after resting our minds and bodies? What if He wants us to follow the example of

Jesus sleeping on a boat in the middle of the storm, trusting our Father with the storms of our life so much so that we can sleep in the midst of the storm?

Most of us associate sanctification with effort: resisting sin, cultivating spiritual habits, doing the right things. And yes, there is a kind of holy discipline in sanctification. But there's also something deeply transformative about doing... nothing. Not nothing in the lazy sense, but a kind of intentional, faith-filled stillness. A choice to stop striving and start trusting. A decision to rest in what Christ has already done, rather than trying to earn what He's already given. This is the paradox of spiritual growth: the more you trust, the more you grow. The more you rest, the more you are transformed.

The Invitation to Rest

One of the passages that radically shifted my understanding of sanctification is found in Hebrews 4:

"There remains, then, a Sabbath-rest for the people of God; for anyone who enters God's rest also rests from their works, just as God did from his. Let us, therefore, make every effort to enter that rest, so that no one will perish by following their example of disobedience." Hebrews 4:9-11

"Make every effort to enter that rest." It sounds almost contradictory. Why would we have to *work* to rest? Because everything in us, and in the world, pushes us toward striving.

- Striving to be good enough.

- Striving to prove ourselves.

- Striving to keep up appearances.

- Striving to grow by willpower.

But the gospel invites us to something different. Something freeing. Something powerful. It invites us to rest in Jesus.

"Come to me, all you who are weary and burdened, and I will give you rest. Take my yoke upon you and learn from me, for I am gentle and humble in heart, and you will find rest for your souls. For my yoke is easy and my burden is light." Matthew 11:28–30

Sanctification begins with Jesus, and it continues with Jesus. He doesn't call you to grow apart from Him, He calls you to abide in Him. Compare the Scripture above with the following:

"To Adam he said, 'Because you listened to your wife and ate fruit from the tree about which I commanded you, 'You must not eat from it,' Cursed is the ground because of you; through painful toil you will eat food from it all the days of your life.'" Genesis 3:17

The curse was to labor and toil in order to live and survive. The invitation from Jesus is for those who are laboring and weary to come and find rest. He is inviting us out of the Curse and into the Promise, out of the Tree of Knowledge of Good and Evil and into the Tree of Life. The Gospel, the Good News, isn't just a golden ticket to heaven; it's an invitation to enter His rest. It's an invitation to bring heaven to earth. It's an invitation to see His kingdom at work in our lives now. It's an invitation to trust Him to change things in us that we cannot change on our own.

Abide and Bear Fruit

In John 15, Jesus gives us one of the most explicit images of restful growth:

"I am the vine; you are the branches. If you remain in me and I in you, you will bear much fruit; apart from me you can do nothing. If you do not remain in me, you are like a branch that is thrown away and withers... This is to my Father's glory, that you bear much fruit, showing yourselves to be my disciples." John 15:5–6a, 8

What is the branch's job? To stay connected. Fruit-bearing is not a result of effort. It's the result of abiding—of remaining in relationship, staying close to Jesus, living in trust and dependence. When we abide, the Spirit flows. When we rest, the fruit grows.

Trying to produce spiritual maturity without abiding in Christ is like a branch trying to bear fruit without sap. It may look religious, but it's empty of power. Picture a dry branch being grafted into a healthy vine and receiving new life. Then, as the branch feels the new life flowing into it, it detaches from the vine to try and bear its own fruit. It's a silly picture, but that's the reality of us getting saved and then trying in our own strength to bear the fruit of the Spirit. The fruit is also produced in its season, not instantly. First, there is the growth of the branch. Then, there is a flower bud. The bud needs help from insects for cross-pollination (which represents our need for being in healthy community with other believers). Then, fruit begins to grow. It begins small and gradually matures. Even in the fruit stage, it must fight off harmful insects and be protected from birds in order to mature. Every step can be related to our spiritual lives. Interestingly, most of the steps depend on the vine to provide nutrients, strength, and resistance to insects and disease. Pollination requires a community, but nothing is required of the branch except that it "abides." The renewing of your mind and the putting on of your new self all takes place while you are abiding in the vine.

Another interesting example is found in the Psalms:

"He says, 'Be still, and know that I am God; I will be exalted among the nations, I will be exalted in the earth.'" Psalm 46:10

The Hebrew word for "be still" is "raphah" (Strong's 7503). Its spelling and pronunciation are similar and related to "Jehovah Rapha" (Strong's 7495), the "Lord who heals:"

"He said, 'If you listen carefully to the Lord your God and do what is right in his eyes, if you pay attention to his commands and keep all his decrees, I will not bring on you any of the diseases I brought on the Egyptians, for I am the Lord, who heals you.'" Exodus 15:26

According to the Strong's Exhaustive Concordance, the "raphah" used in Psalm 46 is defined as follows:

"A primitive root; to slacken (in many applications, literal or figurative) -- abate, cease, consume, draw (toward evening), fail, (be) faint, be (wax) feeble, forsake, idle, leave, let alone (go, down), (be) slack, stay, be still, be slothful, (be) weak(-en)."

And the "rapha" in Exodus is defined as follows:

"Or raphah {raw-faw'}; a primitive root; properly, to mend (by stitching), i.e. (figuratively) to cure -- cure, (cause to) heal, physician, repair, X thoroughly, make whole."

In Hebrew, these words are viewed as complementary opposites. If something is feeble or slack, it needs mending, stitching, or fixing from the Mender or Healer. When we come to "be still" before the Lord, we release our control over our circumstances and recognize that there is a brokenness that needs mending by Jehovah Rapha. As we abide in the Healer, He heals us; but if we continue to try to take care of things ourselves, the Healer will not intervene.

Why Rest Feels Hard

If rest is so essential, why does it feel so unnatural? Because rest requires trust. It forces us to let go of control. It means admitting that we're not the ones holding everything together. It's a surrender of the illusion that we can sanctify ourselves.

When we rest in God's work, we stop building our identity on our performance and start building it on His promises. We stop anxiously measuring our progress and start confidently relying on His presence. We stop striving for perfection and start walking in grace.

"Being confident of this, that he who began a good work in you will carry it on to completion until the day of Christ Jesus." Philippians 1:6

God started the work in you. He will finish it. That doesn't mean you have no part to play, but your part is to cooperate, not to control.

When Jesus is telling His disciples that one of them will betray Him, notice the following responses. First, from the majority:

"They were very sad and began to say to him one after the other, 'Surely you don't mean me, Lord?'" Matthew 26:22

And then, from Judas Iscariot who would betray Him:

"Then Judas, the one who would betray him, said, 'Surely you don't mean me, Rabbi?'Jesus answered, 'You have said so.'" Matthew 26:25

The other disciples had decided Jesus was Lord, but Judas had decided Jesus was just another teacher. We have a different level of trust for our Lord than we do for a teacher. It is possible that our struggle to surrender and trust comes from our honest view of who Jesus is. Do we honestly believe He is the Lord, the Messiah, the Son of God—or do we think He is a good teacher with good morals that we should strive to be like? Your answer to this question will have an impact on your ability to trust Him, especially in difficult times.

Rest Is Not Passivity

To be clear—rest does not mean passivity. It doesn't mean you never read your Bible, pray, repent, or obey. It simply means you do all those things from a place of dependence, not desperation. You don't read Scripture to prove your worth, you read it to hear the voice of your Father. You don't pray to earn points, you pray to abide in His presence. You don't obey to earn love, you obey because you are responding to being loved. This is the rhythm of grace: resting in Christ fuels everything else.

"So then, just as you received Christ Jesus as Lord, continue to live your lives in him, rooted and built up in him, strengthened in the faith as you were taught, and overflowing with thankfulness." Colossians 2:6–7

You received Him by faith, and you continue to walk by that same faith; not by pressure, not by performance, but by trust.

The Freedom of Rest

When you begin to rest in God's work, you'll experience freedom from:

- **Guilt** – You no longer need to punish yourself for not being "there yet."

- **Shame** – You stop hiding and start healing.

- **Comparison** – You stop measuring your walk against someone else's timeline.

- **Burnout** – You stop working *for* love and begin working *from* love.

You'll also experience freedom *for*:

- Joy

- Peace

- Gratitude

- Intimacy with God

- Fruitfulness without fear

This is what Jesus meant when He said, *"My yoke is easy and my burden is light."* He's not asking you to carry the weight of transformation. He has already carried it to the cross. Now He invites you and me to rest in His finished work. This is the Gospel—the marvelous, amazing, spectacular, good news! He didn't just offer us a ticket to heaven, but everything we need to be transformed now, in this life. He has invited us into His rest **"NOW!"** With this news, we can relax and enjoy the ride or the process, even when it gets difficult, because we know it does not depend on us, but on Him, as we abide in Him.

"When he had received the drink, Jesus said, 'It is finished.' With that, he bowed his head and gave up his spirit." John 19:30

"His divine power has given us everything we need for a godly life through our knowledge of him who called us by his own glory and goodness." 2 Peter 1:3

In the Next Chapter...

We'll turn to real-life, biblical examples—starting with Peter—to show how even the most passionate followers of Jesus needed sanctification. If Peter needed correction, restoration, and growth, then there is hope for every one of us too. We'll look at his story and see our own in it.

Make a Difference with Your Review

Share Hope with Someone Else

"Freely you have received; freely give." – Jesus, Matthew 10:8

When you give without asking for anything back, God uses that to bless others — and He blesses you too.

Would you help someone like you, who wants to grow in their faith but feels stuck?

My heart in writing *Bringing Heaven to Earth* was to make growing closer to Jesus easier, lighter, and more real. But I need your help to share that hope.

Many people pick books because of the reviews. That means your words can help someone just like you find freedom, peace, and the love of God.

It doesn't cost anything and takes only a minute, but it can change a life. Your review could help...

...one more believer break free from shame.

...one more seeker find the love of Jesus.

...one more church grow in grace, not performance.

...one more family build their faith together.

...one more heart feel safe to be in process.

If you'd like to make a difference, please scan the QR code below and leave a short review. It means so much — thank you for sharing grace with someone else!

Sincerely,

David Powell

Part III:

The Witness of Imperfect Saints

The Bible is like God's diary of His interaction with humans—from creation through the time of the Apostles and the beginning of the New Testament Church. Since the Holy Spirit was promised to Believers in the New Testament, our understanding and first insights on sanctification come through the lives of these New Testament believers. Here we will examine just a few of these believers to get a picture of sanctification at work in the early church.

CHAPTER 10

PETER — FROM PASSION TO HYPOCRISY TO RESTORATION

Peter's story is beloved by many, and for good reason. He was bold, outspoken, and fiercely loyal. He walked on water. He declared Jesus the Messiah. He promised to follow Him to the death. And yet, just hours after making that promise, he denied Jesus three times. Peter's life is a powerful example of sanctification in real time. He shows us that failure doesn't disqualify us from growth, that hypocrisy is not the end, and that grace is available even when we mess up repeatedly.

The Highs and Lows of Peter

Peter's journey with Jesus began with a simple call:

"'Come, follow me,' Jesus said, 'and I will send you out to fish for people.' At once they left their nets and followed him." Matthew 4:19–20

Peter followed Jesus with enthusiasm. He was the first to speak, the first to step out of the boat (Matthew 14), the first to say:

"You are the Messiah, the Son of the living God." Matthew 16:16

But he was also the first to correct Jesus (*"Never, Lord!"*), the one who fell asleep in the Garden of Gethsemane, the one who drew a sword when Jesus was surrendering to His arrest, and the one who denied Jesus—not once—but three times. Peter's highs were very high, and his lows were heartbreakingly low. That's sanctification.

Peter's Greatest Failure

On the night Jesus was arrested, Peter's identity crisis reached its peak.

Despite his bold words, fear overtook him. He followed Jesus from a distance, and then denied knowing Him when pressed by strangers.

"Then he began to call down curses, and he swore to them, 'I don't know the man!' Immediately a rooster crowed. Then Peter remembered the word Jesus had spoken: 'Before the rooster crows, you will disown me three times.' And he went outside and wept bitterly." Matthew 26:74–75

He wept bitterly. That phrase speaks volumes. Peter wasn't just embarrassed, he was devastated. He knew he had failed. Deep down, maybe he wondered if he'd blown his one chance at following Jesus. But Jesus wasn't finished with Peter, not even close.

Jesus Restores Peter

After the resurrection, Jesus didn't avoid Peter. He pursued him.

"But go, tell his disciples and Peter, 'He is going ahead of you into Galilee. There you will see him, just as he told you.'" Mark 16:7

One morning on the shore, Peter saw the risen Jesus cooking breakfast over a fire. And in that moment, something beautiful happened:

"When they had finished eating, Jesus said to Simon Peter, 'Simon son of John, do you love me more than these?' 'Yes, Lord,' he said, 'you know that I love you.' Jesus said, 'Feed my lambs.'" John 21:15

Jesus asked the same question three times, matching Peter's three denials. Not to shame him, but to restore him. To reaffirm his calling. To rebuild the foundation. Jesus didn't say, *"Peter, are you sorry enough?"* He didn't say, *"Peter, can you promise to never fail again?"* He said, *"Do you love me?"* And that is the heart of sanctification: not perfection, but love. Love that grows. Love that returns after failure. Love that learns to trust grace.

Peter Was Still in Process

Even after this powerful restoration, Peter still had growing to do. Years later, Paul confronted Peter publicly for acting hypocritically:

"When Cephas(Peter) came to Antioch, I opposed him to his face, because he stood condemned. For before certain men came from James, he used to eat with the Gentiles. But when they arrived, he began to draw back and separate himself from the Gentiles because he was afraid of those who belonged to the circumcision group. The other Jews joined him in his hypocrisy, so that by their hypocrisy even Barnabas was led astray." Galatians 2:11–13

Peter—the one who had walked with Jesus, seen the resurrection, and been filled with the Holy Spirit—still struggled with fear and people-pleasing. He still needed sanctification. But God didn't discard him. He allowed him to be corrected, refined, and humbled while continuing to use him mightily. Later in life, Peter would write these words:

"But grow in the grace and knowledge of our Lord and Savior Jesus Christ. To him be glory both now and forever! Amen." 2 Peter 3:18

He had learned the lesson firsthand. Growth is ongoing. Grace is essential.

What We Learn from Peter

Peter's story teaches us that:

- **Sanctification is not linear** – You can have amazing spiritual highs and still fall. That doesn't mean you're disqualified.

- **God uses broken people** – Jesus didn't choose Peter because he was perfect. He chose him because he was willing to learn surrender.

- **Failure is not the end** – Peter's worst moment became a turning point for deeper humility and dependence.

- **Correction is part of growth** – Sanctification includes being corrected—even publicly—and learning from it.

- **Love is the foundation** – At the core of sanctification is not discipline, but love for Jesus.

If you've ever felt like you've failed too many times...If you've ever felt like you should be further along by now...If you've ever felt hypocritical, weak, or unqualified...Remember Peter. Remember that Jesus didn't give up on him, and He won't give up on you.

In the Next Chapter...

We'll look at the story of Paul and John Mark, a powerful example of two people both being sanctified in very different ways. One needed to grow in patience, while the other needed to grow in perseverance—and God used both of them.

CHAPTER 11

PAUL AND JOHN MARK — GROWTH ON BOTH SIDES

Sanctification is not a solo journey. It often occurs within the context of relationships. Sometimes God uses conflict, disappointment, or even separation to shape us into the image of Christ. And nowhere is this more clear than in the story of Paul and John Mark. One was a seasoned apostle. The other was a young helper. Their relationship started well, hit a painful split, and eventually came full circle—showing that both men were still in process, both had room to grow, and both were deeply useful to God.

The Sharp Disagreement

The story begins in the book of Acts. Paul and Barnabas were preparing for a second missionary journey. Barnabas wanted to take his cousin John Mark with them again. Paul was opposed because John Mark had previously abandoned them on an earlier mission:

"Some time later Paul said to Barnabas, 'Let us go back and visit the believers in all the towns where we preached the word of the Lord and see how they are doing.' Barnabas wanted to take John, also called Mark, with them, but Paul did not think it wise to take him, because he had deserted them in Pamphylia and had not continued with them

in the work. They had such a sharp disagreement that they parted company. Barnabas took Mark and sailed for Cyprus, but Paul chose Silas and left, commended by the believers to the grace of the Lord." Acts 15:36–40

"Such a sharp disagreement that they parted company." These weren't immature believers. Paul and Barnabas were both spiritual giants. Yet they disagreed so intensely over John Mark's past failure that they went their separate ways. From the outside, this may appear to be a failure. But in God's sovereignty, it became a moment of sanctification for everyone involved.

John Mark's Journey of Maturity

We don't know exactly why John Mark left the mission field the first time. Maybe he was afraid. Maybe he missed home. Maybe the work was harder than he expected. Whatever the reason, Paul saw it as desertion whereas Barnabas saw something else—potential. He chose to take Mark with him, even at the cost of parting with Paul. This is the beauty of sanctification: God often puts people in our lives who see the version of us we could be, not just the version we've been.

Barnabas believed in Mark when Paul couldn't. And that belief helped John Mark (also referred to as "Mark" in later epistles) grow. Years later, we see the fruit of that growth. Paul writes:

"Only Luke is with me. Get Mark and bring him with you, because he is helpful to me in my ministry." 2 Timothy 4:11

What a turnaround. The same Paul who once refused to take Mark along now calls him *"helpful to me in my ministry."* Mark had matured. He didn't stay stuck in his earlier failure. With time, grace, and godly mentorship, he became a valuable part of God's work. In fact, most scholars agree that this is the same John Mark who went on to write the Gospel of Mark. God didn't waste his failure; He used it to shape him into a man of wisdom, faith, and endurance.

Paul's Growth in Grace

But Mark wasn't the only one who grew, Paul did too. When he first refused to take Mark, Paul was likely motivated by a sense of mission, responsibility, and wisdom. He didn't want to risk another abandonment on the field. Yet over time, Paul softened. He came to value Mark again, not just as a co-laborer, but as a brother. This is sanctification at work. Paul grew in his ability to extend grace. He grew in relational humility. He learned to see people not just through the lens of past performance, but through the lens of God's redemptive power. That's not a small thing. Even spiritual maturity must be sanctified. Sometimes our greatest growth doesn't come through success, but through seeing someone else's redemption and realizing we were wrong to give up on them.

Lessons for Us

This story presents a beautiful portrayal of sanctification occurring on both sides of a relationship.

For those who feel like John Mark:

- Maybe you've walked away from a calling.

- Maybe you've disappointed someone you respect.

- Maybe you've wondered if God can still use you.

He can. And He will. God is not done with you. You're still in process. What appears to be a failure now can become the soil for future fruitfulness.

For those who feel like Paul:

- Maybe someone you trusted let you down.

- Maybe you've had to part ways with a friend, ministry partner, or even a family member.

- Maybe you've written someone off.

Don't underestimate what God can do in their life, and in yours. Even your discernment can be refined. Even your judgment can be sanctified. Even your leadership can grow in grace. And one day, like Paul, you may find yourself saying, *"He is helpful to me in ministry."*

God's Sovereign Hand

God used a painful disagreement to multiply ministry. Instead of one missionary team, there were now two. Over time, the wounds were healed, the stories redeemed, and the relationships restored. This is how sanctification often works. Not through perfect plans, but through messy moments. Not through constant agreement, but through God's patient work in imperfect people.

In the Next Chapter...

We'll turn to another example in Apollos, a man who loved God but was still unaware of the full truth. His story reveals how sanctification often includes learning from others, especially when we're already passionate or gifted. We'll see how humility and teachability are essential to the growth process.

CHAPTER 12

APOLLOS — THE POWER OF HUMBLE GROWTH

There's a certain kind of sanctification that doesn't begin with failure or moral collapse, but with limited understanding. Some people enter ministry with charisma and conviction, but are missing parts of the gospel. Others follow Jesus sincerely, but their knowledge is incomplete. Still others teach the truth boldly, but unknowingly leave out essential elements. That was Apollos. He was a gifted speaker, well-versed in Scripture, and passionate about God. But there was more he needed to learn. And the way he responded when correction came reveals a heart posture that every believer should strive for: humility.

Meet Apollos

We first meet Apollos in Acts 18:

"Meanwhile a Jew named Apollos, a native of Alexandria, came to Ephesus. He was a learned man, with a thorough knowledge of the Scriptures. He had been instructed in the way of the Lord, and he spoke with great fervor and taught about Jesus accurately, though he knew only the baptism of John." Acts 18:24–25

Apollos had many of the qualities we admire in spiritual leaders:

- Deep knowledge of Scripture

- Passion for truth

- Eloquence

- Boldness

- Sincerity

But his understanding was incomplete. Luke writes:

"He had been instructed in the way of the Lord, and he spoke with great fervor and taught about Jesus accurately, though he knew only the baptism of John." Acts 18:25

This phrase is so important. Apollos wasn't spreading heresy. He wasn't insincere. He simply didn't yet understand the full picture. He likely didn't know about the baptism of the Holy Spirit and the completed work of Christ's death and resurrection, all of which are very important in the process of sanctification. And God, in His kindness, didn't leave him there.

Priscilla and Aquila Step In

Enter two quiet heroes of the New Testament, Priscilla and Aquila. This husband-and-wife team had worked alongside Paul and were mature in their faith. When they heard Apollos teach, they didn't publicly rebuke him or challenge his platform. Instead, they invited him into a relationship.

"He began to speak boldly in the synagogue. When Priscilla and Aquila heard him, they invited him to their home and explained to him the way of God more adequately." Acts 18:26

What a beautiful picture of both grace and truth. They didn't shame him. They didn't disqualify him. They simply helped him see what he was missing. And here's what's even more powerful—Apollos received it. He didn't let pride get in the way. He didn't defend his credentials. He didn't walk away offended. He listened. He learned. He grew. This is sanctification in motion.

Growth Requires Teachability

Apollos teaches us that being right in most things doesn't mean we're done growing. You can be biblically solid and still have gaps in your understanding. You can be passionate about Jesus and still need correction. You can be deeply gifted and still lack insight. The mark of spiritual maturity isn't always what you know; sometimes, it's how open you are to being taught.

Paul writes:

"Do not think of yourself more highly than you ought, but rather think of yourself with sober judgment, in accordance with the faith God has distributed to each of you." Romans 12:3

In our culture, confidence is celebrated. But in the kingdom, *humility is the path to wisdom.*

"God opposes the proud but shows favor to the humble." James 4:6

Apollos had every reason to ignore the counsel of two tentmakers. But he didn't. He humbled himself, opened his heart, and received what they shared with him. As a result, he became even more effective for the gospel.

The Fruit of Humility

The very next verse shows the outcome of Apollos' teachability:

"When Apollos wanted to go to Achaia, the brothers and sisters encouraged him and wrote to the disciples there to welcome him. When he arrived, he was a great help to those who by grace had believed. For he vigorously refuted his Jewish opponents in public debate, proving from the Scriptures that Jesus was the Messiah." Acts 18:27–28

He didn't just grow in knowledge; he also grew in wisdom. He grew in impact. His humility didn't make him weaker; it made him stronger. God used him to strengthen others, defend the faith, and point people to Jesus with even greater clarity. This is what sanctification does: it strengthens the voice, clarifies the message, and deepens the fruit. This often comes not through crisis, but through quiet correction and humble learning.

Lessons from Apollos

What can we learn from Apollos?

- **Zeal is not the same as maturity** – Passion is beautiful, but it must be shaped by truth.

- **Being accurate isn't the same as being complete** – You can teach truth and still miss important pieces.

- **The best leaders are the most teachable** – Growth comes not just from what we know, but from what we're willing to learn.

- **Correction should come in relationship** – Priscilla and Aquila modeled grace and truth by correcting gently and privately.

- **Sanctification includes theological growth** – Sometimes God sanctifies us not just morally, but doctrinally.

Apollos was already effective when he was first introduced in Scripture, but his teachability made him even more powerful in God's hands.

In the Next Chapter...

We'll see that the process of sanctification is for all God's children, regardless of gender, background, trauma, acceptance by the religious majority, or any other obstacle.

CHAPTER 13

MARY MAGDALENE — FROM DARKNESS TO DEVOTION

When we talk about sanctification—the ongoing work of becoming more like Jesus—Mary Magdalene gives us one of the most powerful pictures of transformation in the New Testament. Her story begins in deep spiritual darkness, and yet she becomes one of the first witnesses of the resurrection. Her life illustrates not only how Jesus delivers us from bondage, but how He patiently walks with us through misunderstanding, grief, and growth.

Delivered, Not Disqualified

We first meet Mary Magdalene in Luke 8, where she is described as one of the women who had been healed by Jesus:

"...and also some women who had been cured of evil spirits and diseases: Mary (called Magdalene) from whom seven demons had come out." *Luke 8:2*

Seven demons. We don't know all the details, but clearly Mary had been through torment. She had been spiritually broken, likely emotionally devastated, and socially isolated. Yet Jesus didn't avoid her—He healed her. He called her. He welcomed her into His ministry circle. That's how sanctification begins: with grace, not merit. Mary had nothing to offer but brokenness. And Jesus met her there.

A Heart of Devotion

After her deliverance, Mary became a devoted follower of Jesus. She was part of the group that supported His ministry out of their own means (Luke 8:3). She didn't just receive freedom—she followed with faithfulness. She walked the long road to Jerusalem. She watched from a distance His crucifixion when most of the disciples had fled. Even in death, she stayed near.

"Mary Magdalene and the other Mary were sitting there opposite the tomb." Matthew 27:61

This is the fruit of sanctification. Not perfection. Not complete understanding. But a heart that stays close to Jesus—even when things don't make sense.

Grief, Confusion, and Grace

On resurrection morning, we find Mary again—this time in deep grief. She arrives early at the tomb, finds the stone rolled away, and assumes the worst.

"They have taken the Lord out of the tomb, and we don't know where they have put him!" John 20:2

She runs to tell Peter and John, and then she returns to the tomb, weeping. She sees angels, but still doesn't grasp what has happened. Then Jesus Himself appears—and she still doesn't recognize Him. She thinks He's the gardener.

"She turned around and saw Jesus standing there, but she did not realize that it was Jesus." John 20:14

Pause here. This is so human. So real. Here is a woman who had followed Jesus, served Him, and loved Him deeply—but she's still in process. She's grieving. She's confused. She doesn't yet understand the resurrection. And Jesus doesn't rebuke her for that. He calls her by name.

"Jesus said to her, 'Mary.' She turned toward him and cried out in Aramaic, 'Rabboni!' (which means 'Teacher'). " John 20:16

That one word—her name—cut through the fog. This is sanctification. This is grace. Jesus meets us in our confusion and gently reminds us who we are and who He is.

Commissioned, Not Condemned

Instead of correcting her confusion with frustration, Jesus gives her an assignment. He entrusts her with the message of the resurrection:

"Go instead to my brothers and tell them, 'I am ascending to my Father and your Father, to my God and your God.'" John 20:17

Mary becomes the first person to proclaim the risen Christ. A woman once bound by seven demons becomes the first evangelist of the resurrection. Not because she understood everything perfectly. Not because she never made a mistake. But because she loved Jesus—and Jesus trusted her with the most important news in all of history.

Still Becoming

Mary's story doesn't give us a tidy formula for spiritual growth. It gives us a journey. A woman who was once in deep bondage becomes a devoted disciple. A disciple who doesn't always get it right, but who keeps showing up. And Jesus keeps meeting her. Healing her. Commissioning her.

That's sanctification. Not a straight line. But a life shaped by grace, one step at a time.

In the Next Chapter...

We'll pause to reflect more personally. So far, we've explored the theology of sanctification and seen how it plays out in the lives of real people. Now we will turn inward, focusing on what it means to be free, to be in process, and on how vulnerability—not perfection—creates space for genuine growth and genuine community.

PART IV:

LIVING THE PROCESS IN FREEDOM

If we stop and think about it, one of the things that frustrated the Pharisees the most about Jesus and His followers was their freedom. The Pharisees had spent their lives focusing their attention on their actions and observing (at least outwardly) every commandment and tradition that had been passed down. Then Jesus shows up and He is healing on the Sabbath, allowing His disciples to pick and eat grain on the Sabbath, and He even talks to and eats with Samaritans and "sinners." He practically mocks their traditions of ritual washing, telling them they aren't contaminated from what goes into the mouth, but by what comes out of their mouth. If Jesus were physically walking with us today, would we respond as the Pharisees? Would He seem to mock our religious efforts and actions, while going and speaking to and eating with the "sinners" that we judge? Would we feel as offended as the Pharisees did by hearing His judgment of our inner thoughts and weaknesses, which we have tried so hard to hide from people around us and even ourselves?

In my short time of embracing this journey with a new understanding, I have found many honest and struggling people—both believers and unbelievers—drawn to me. At the same time, I have found that many people who are stuck in religion, performance, and people-pleasing are offended by my freedom and vulnerability. It somehow threatens their make-believe world of safety being based on their performance; but I understand, because I spent most of my life in that place too. I now long for them to join me in freedom. If that might be you, if you are feeling some offense and defensive arguments are rising in your mind, I encourage you to remember:

"It is for freedom that Christ has set us free. Stand firm, then, and do not let yourselves be burdened again by a yoke of slavery." Galatians 5:1

CHAPTER 14

FREE TO BE IN PROCESS

One of the most damaging lies in the church is this: *"You have to have it all together."* Whether spoken or implied, this message has pushed countless believers into hiding. It has led to surface-level conversations, performative spirituality, and deep internal shame. But sanctification doesn't happen in hiding. It happens in the light. And the good news of the gospel is this: you are free to be in process. You don't have to be perfect. You don't have to pretend. You don't have to hide the fact that you're still becoming who God says you are.

Vulnerability Is the Starting Point

Growth begins where honesty begins. When we stop pretending, the Holy Spirit can begin to heal. Jesus said:

"Then you will know the truth, and the truth will set you free." John 8:32

But before truth can set you free, it has to reach the real you, not the version you show other people. Not the version you perform on Sundays. Not the Instagram version. The real you. The struggling, doubting, inconsistent, and still-learning you. That's the person Jesus died for. That's the person the Holy Spirit wants to sanctify. And that's the person the world needs to see—not a polished, performance-driven Christian—but a real, vulnerable one who is growing in grace.

"But he said to me, 'My grace is sufficient for you, for my power is made perfect in weakness.' Therefore, I will boast all the more gladly about my weaknesses, so that Christ's power may rest on me." 2 Corinthians 12:9

Paul didn't hide his weakness; he boasted in it. Not to glorify sin, but to glorify the grace of God that meets us in our mess.

Hiding Halts Growth

Many of us spend substantial energy trying to appear better than we are. We measure our words carefully. We filter our confessions. We often avoid vulnerability out of fear of being judged, rejected, or misunderstood. But here's the reality: hiding doesn't protect you, it isolates you—and isolation is where sin thrives.

John writes:

"But if we walk in the light, as he is in the light, we have fellowship with one another, and the blood of Jesus, his Son, purifies us from all sin." 1 John 1:7

Did you catch that? *"We have fellowship... and the blood of Jesus purifies..."* Community and cleansing are linked. Walking in the light doesn't just mean confessing to God, it means letting others see our authentic selves so that they can walk with us and speak grace to us. When we stop hiding the healing process begins.

The Danger of Remaining in Performance

If we continue to try to "earn" or "merit" our salvation that we received by faith based on our "performance," it leads us into a dangerous place. It is as if we were just grafted into the vine, and then we detach ourselves to try and produce fruit. The Holy Spirit was kind enough to show me the results of this in my own life. As I tried to earn, merit, and become worthy of my salvation, it led to comparison. How can you know the value of your work and merit unless you compare it to those around you? Once you start comparing, it leads immediately to judgment. We judge others to make ourselves feel more worthy. Once we start judging others, we can no longer love them. In our best efforts, we cannot love the people that we are judging. In the end, we become the perfect Pharisee—cleaning the outside of the vessel with performance while the inside remains filthy and unchanged. Or we might end up even worse than when we started.

"Woe to you, teachers of the law and Pharisees, you hypocrites! You travel over land and sea to win a single convert, and when you have succeeded, you make them twice as much a child of hell as you are." Matthew 23:15

"Woe to you, teachers of the law and Pharisees, you hypocrites! You clean the outside of the cup and dish, but inside they are full of greed and self-indulgence. Blind Pharisee! First, clean the inside of the cup and dish, and then the outside will also be clean. Woe to you, teachers of the law and Pharisees, you hypocrites! You are like whitewashed tombs, which look beautiful on the outside but on the inside are full of the bones of the dead and everything unclean. In the same way, on the outside you appear to people as righteous but on the inside you are full of hypocrisy and wickedness." Matthew 23:25-28

You Don't Have to Impress People

Much of our pressure to perform stems from the desire to compare ourselves to others.

We look around and think:

- *"She's so much further along than I am."*

- *"He never seems to struggle like I do."*

- *"If they really knew what I was like, they'd be disappointed."*

But comparison always distorts reality. You don't know the whole story behind anyone's life. You don't see the quiet tears, the silent prayers, the late-night regrets. Everyone is in process. Everyone is being sanctified. And you don't need to impress anyone—not your pastor, your small group, your family, or even yourself. God is not impressed by appearances either. He died for you while you were still a sinner.

"But God demonstrates his own love for us in this: While we were still sinners, Christ died for us." Romans 5:8

He's drawn to the humble.

"The Lord is close to the brokenhearted and saves those who are crushed in spirit." Psalm 34:18

"He mocks proud mockers but shows favor to the humble and oppressed." Proverbs 3:34

He is not asking for perfection. He's asking for honesty.

Vulnerability Makes Space for Others

Here's something beautiful: when you stop pretending, you give others permission to stop pretending too. Your honesty creates safety. Your openness invites freedom. Your willingness to share your process helps others believe God can work in their process too.

I've seen this firsthand. For years, I thought I had to be the "strong" one, the missionary, the teacher, the one who always had a verse ready and a prayer on hand... But the most transformative moments in my relationships didn't come from teaching others; they came from confessing to them. From saying, *"I'm struggling too."* And that's when people would lean in, not because I was perfect, but because I was real. That's when walls come down. That's when hearts soften. That's when sanctification becomes not just a private journey, but a shared one.

The Church Needs the Real You

What if the church became a place where:

- it was *safe* to struggle?

- leaders could admit their weakness?

- newcomers weren't expected to have it all together?

- accountability wasn't about fear, but about grace?

- people were expected to be in the process?

This is what the body of Christ is meant to be: a community of imperfect people learning to love a perfect Savior, and to love each other through the mess.

"Carry each other's burdens, and in this way you will fulfill the law of Christ." Galatians 6:2

You can't carry a burden you don't know about. And no one can carry yours if you keep it hidden. So be honest. Be vulnerable. Be in process. That's where freedom is. That's where grace flows. That's where sanctification thrives. This is not an excuse to continue in sin; quite the contrary, it is a call to love accountability and help.

In the Next Chapter...

We'll examine how grace, rather than guilt, fuels genuine change. We'll explore the difference between conviction and condemnation, and how walking in grace sets us free to pursue holiness without fear or shame.

CHAPTER 15

GRACE OVER GUILT

Have you ever walked away from a sermon, a prayer time, or a Bible reading feeling worse instead of more hopeful? There's a good chance you were carrying something God never asked you to carry—guilt. Not conviction. Not godly sorrow. Just shame. And it's keeping you stuck. For many believers, guilt becomes a default response to spiritual failure. We feel it when we make a mistake. We assume it's proof of our sincerity. We let it motivate our repentance. But guilt can't produce the kind of lasting change God desires. Only grace can do that.

Guilt vs. Conviction

Let's start by making a key distinction. Guilt and shame say:

- *"You're not enough."*

- *"You're a disappointment."*

- *"You're dirty. Broken. Disqualified."*

That is not exactly the encouragement we need to move forward into transformation. Conviction, on the other hand, is the gentle, firm nudge of the Holy Spirit saying: *"That's not who you are. Come back. Let Me restore you."*

Paul explains the difference clearly in 2 Corinthians:

"Godly sorrow brings repentance that leads to salvation and leaves no regret, but worldly sorrow brings death." 2 Corinthians 7:10

Worldly sorrow (guilt) leads to despair and distance. Godly sorrow (conviction) leads to repentance and renewal. If you feel hopeless, ashamed, or like you'll never change, that's not the voice of God. If you feel drawn to repentance, restoration, and grace, that's the Spirit at work. As mentioned earlier, not every voice that comes into our head should be listened to. Which voice have you been listening to, the one that leads to shame and hopelessness, or the one that leads to restoration and life?

"Therefore, there is now no condemnation for those who are in Christ Jesus, because through Christ Jesus the law of the Spirit who gives life has set you free from the law of sin and death." Romans 8:1–2

Let those words sink in: "no condemnation." That's your inheritance as a child of God.

Guilt Is a Terrible Motivator

Some of us were raised in church environments where guilt was used as fuel.

- *"Don't you care what God thinks?"*

- *"After everything He's done for you, you're still struggling?"*

- *"You call yourself a Christian?"*

These voices, whether internal or external, may have been intended to motivate repentance; but they often lead to hiding, burnout, or deep-seated insecurity. Here's why: Guilt leads to behavior management. Grace leads to heart transformation. Behavior management says, *"Try harder. Do better. Perform."* Heart transformation says, *"Return to God. Trust Him. Let Him change you."* And only heart transformation lasts.

Grace Doesn't Excuse Sin—It Empowers Holiness

Some people worry that preaching grace too much will lead to compromise. They fear that if people really believe they're forgiven, they'll stop caring about sin. But the opposite is true. When grace truly touches your heart, it doesn't lower the standard; it lifts your eyes to the Savior who fulfilled it for you. And that love compels you to live differently.

"For the grace of God has appeared that offers salvation to all people. It teaches us to say 'No' to ungodliness and worldly passions, and to live self-controlled, upright and godly lives in this present age." Titus *2:11–12*

Grace doesn't give you permission to sin. It gives you the power to resist it. That's the paradox—grace does what guilt never can. Guilt says, *"You better change, or else."* Grace says, *"God is changing you, and you're not alone."* Guilt chains you to the past. Grace anchors you in your identity. Guilt breeds fear. Grace births love.

"There is no fear in love. But perfect love drives out fear, because fear has to do with punishment. The one who fears is not made perfect in love." 1 John 4:18

Forgiven and Free

If you've been carrying guilt over your failures, especially any repeated ones, then this is your invitation to lay that guilt down. Jesus has already carried it for you.

"If we confess our sins, he is faithful and just and will forgive us our sins and purify us from all unrighteousness." 1 John 1:9

He doesn't just forgive. He purifies. He cleanses. He restores. You don't have to beg Him to do it. You just have to come. Some of us feel like we have to prove we're sorry enough, that we need to keep feeling guilty for a while, as a kind of self-inflicted penance. But that's not repentance—that's punishment. Jesus already took the punishment. Repentance isn't about staying stuck in guilt; it's about walking freely into grace, changing the way I think to agree with what God says about me. When I understand who I am in Christ, it changes the way I behave. My identity will always shape my behavior.

Walking in Grace

So, how do we live in grace without abusing it? Here's the key: we remember that grace is not just a past event (what saved us), and not just a future hope (what gets us to heaven). Grace is also our present power.

"Let us then approach God's throne of grace with confidence, so that we may receive mercy and find grace to help us in our time of need." Hebrews 4:16

Grace is available "in your time of need," not just when you feel spiritual and not just when you're doing well. It is available in your mess. In your weakness. In your failure. That's when grace shows up and reminds you: *You are still loved. You are still chosen. And I'm not finished with you yet.*

Grace says:

- *"Yes, you failed. But that's not your identity."*

- *"Yes, you sinned. But you're still my child."*

- *"Yes, you need help. And help is here."*

That's the voice of the Shepherd. That's the power of grace.

In the Next Chapter...

We'll examine what it truly means to live a sanctified life; not a perfect life, but a life characterized by the fruit of the Spirit, increasing maturity, and a growing capacity to love others well. We'll see how sanctification isn't just about us. It's about how our transformed lives become a witness to the world.

Chapter 16

Heaven on Earth — A Sanctified Life

What does a sanctified life look like? It does not look like a perfect life. Not like a sinless life. But a changed life. A life that reflects heaven on earth. A sanctified life is one where people don't just hear the gospel from your lips, but they *see* it in your character. It's a life that grows in love, peace, kindness, and strength. A life that turns heads not because it's loud or flashy, but because it's quietly different. And the goal of sanctification isn't just to improve you, it's to reveal Christ in you.

"Christ in you, the hope of glory." Colossians 1:27b

This is what it means to bring heaven to earth.

The Visible Fruit of Transformation

Sanctification is an inward work, but it produces outward evidence. Paul gives us one of the clearest pictures of this in Galatians:

"But the fruit of the Spirit is love, joy, peace, forbearance, kindness, goodness, faithfulness, gentleness and self-control. Against such things there is no law." Galatians 5:22–23

Notice he calls them fruit, not effort. These qualities are the natural result of the Spirit working within you when you abide in the vine. You can't force fruit. You can't fake it for long. You can't manufacture it through discipline alone. But you can cultivate it.

You cultivate fruit when you remain in Christ, when you surrender your will, when you renew your mind, when you walk in the Spirit, when you rest in grace, and when you choose a healthy environment, healthy relationships, and healthy input. Over time, that slow, quiet work of the Spirit begins to produce visible change:

- You respond with gentleness instead of defensiveness.

- You forgive more quickly.

- You notice others' pain.

- You speak with more grace.

- You feel genuine joy, sometimes for no reason other than the presence of God in you.

This is the sanctified life: one where the character of Jesus becomes increasingly evident through us.

Not Just Behavior—But Love

Paul says something profound in 1 Corinthians 13:

"If I speak in the tongues of men or of angels, but do not have love, I am only a resounding gong or a clanging cymbal." 1 Corinthians 13:1

You can be spiritually gifted, doctrinally sound, and outwardly disciplined; but if you don't have love, it's empty. The ultimate evidence of sanctification is not knowledge, status, charisma, or power. It's love.

"Whoever claims to live in him must live as Jesus did." 1 John 2:6

And how did Jesus live?

- With compassion for the outcast.

- With grace for the sinner.

- With gentleness for the broken.

- With patience for the slow-to-learn.

- With the courage to speak the truth.

- With joy, even in suffering.

- With humility, even in glory.

That's the shape of a sanctified life.

Growing in Maturity

The writer of Hebrews talks about spiritual maturity as a sign of growth:

"Anyone who lives on milk, being still an infant, is not acquainted with the teaching about righteousness. But solid food is for the mature, who by constant use have trained themselves to distinguish good from evil." Hebrews 5:13–14

Sanctification leads to discernment. It helps you recognize when a thought, habit, or response is rooted in the Spirit or the flesh. It enables you to filter decisions through the lens of eternity. It helps you respond to people with wisdom and grace, rather than impulsively and emotionally. And that maturity is not just for your benefit; it blesses the people around you.

As you grow in sanctification, you become:

- A better spouse

- A more gracious parent

- A more dependable friend

- A more trustworthy leader

- A more compassionate neighbor

A Life That Points to Jesus

Jesus said:

"Let your light shine before others, that they may see your good deeds and glorify your Father in heaven." Matthew 5:16

A sanctified life isn't about drawing attention to ourselves; it's about reflecting the nature of the One who lives within us. People may not remember your theology. They may not agree with your worldview. But they'll never forget how you made them feel. They'll never forget the love, patience, and grace you extended when it wasn't deserved. And when they ask how— how you stay calm, how you forgive, how you love so freely—you can point them to the One who's been transforming you all along.

"But in your hearts revere Christ as Lord. Always be prepared to give an answer to everyone who asks you to give the reason for the hope that you have. But do this with gentleness and respect." 1 Peter 3:15

Your Life Is a Testimony

Your sanctified life is a sermon. A parable. A living invitation. Not to you, but to Christ. You're not perfect, but you're being changed. And that change is the evidence that Jesus is real, powerful, and alive. The world doesn't need more impressive Christians. It needs more transformed ones. And transformation isn't flashy. It's quiet. Steady. Humble. But unmistakable.

"The path of the righteous is like the morning sun, shining ever brighter till the full light of day." Proverbs 4:18

In the Next Section...

We'll wrap up the core message of this book with some final reflections. We'll revisit the idea that sanctification is a process—not a performance—and that the more we embrace our dependence on the Holy Spirit, the more we reflect God's glory in our daily lives. This, in turn, will help us love others and give them more grace. In the end, it all comes back to the Garden of Eden, as you'll see in the final chapter.

PART V:

CONCLUSION - FINAL THOUGHTS

As I've walked through this process in a deeper way these last few years, I can see myself changing. I genuinely feel love and compassion for those who are lost, who have not understood or accepted the grace of our loving Savior. I find myself honestly interceding for religious people around me because I understand their judgmental and condemning ways. I long for them to experience the freedom that I now feel. Even when I am with people who talk about human trafficking and how they wish the worst on the people who do such things, I find myself correcting them and saying, "No, I hope they learn about God's love for them. I'm certain they have trauma from their childhood that has led them to the place they are in now. God hates the sin, but He loves the Trafficker as much as the one being trafficked."

Even members of my family have talked about the difference they see in me. This is the result of surrendering to the process instead of fighting and resisting it, or worse yet, pretending to already have arrived. My prayer is that through reading this book, you will embrace the journey and cooperate with the Holy Spirit in your process of sanctification. I pray that more young people can experience freedom earlier in life as they see those of us who are older become vulnerable about our processes. In these last chapters, I offer a few final thoughts to sum it all up.

CHAPTER 17

I'M STILL BECOMING

If you've made it to this chapter, I want you to hear this clearly: You are not behind. You are not failing. You are becoming. Sanctification is not a test to pass. It's not a finish line to reach. It's a relationship with the God who loves you so much that He refuses to leave you the way He found you—and He's in it for the long haul.

"Being confident of this, that he who began a good work in you will carry it on to completion until the day of Christ Jesus." Philippians 1:6

That means today, tomorrow, and every day after, you're:

- Still being shaped.

- Still being healed.

- Still being softened.

- Still being made whole.

- Still becoming more like Jesus.

That verse doesn't say the work is complete today. It says He *"will carry it on."* That's a promise. And it means that you and I can stop living as if the outcome depends on us. It doesn't. It never did.

After more than thirty years of ministry filled with decades of preaching, praying, leading, and serving, I found myself realizing how much I was yet to understand about the grace of God, about His patience, and about how transformation really works. I used to think sanctification was something I could manage if I tried hard enough. Now I know that it's something only the Holy Spirit can do in me. And my job is to keep showing up, to keep surrendering, and to keep trusting that He hasn't given up on me.

Even after decades in ministry, I still have to remind myself that I haven't arrived. I'm still in process. And that's not a disqualification—it's a gift, because I've come to know God more deeply in the process. I've learned that His love isn't based on my performance and that His grace doesn't run out when I mess up. I've discovered the freedom of vulnerability, the kind of honesty that invites others to be honest too. I've seen that when I stop pretending and start trusting, the Holy Spirit steps in and does what I could never do on my own. And I've learned that sanctification isn't about becoming a perfect Christian, it's about learning to trust the Perfect One who lives in me.

"We all, who with unveiled faces contemplate the Lord's glory, are being transformed into his image with ever-increasing glory, which comes from the Lord, who is the Spirit." 2 Corinthians 3:18

"Being transformed." That means the work is still ongoing, and the glory is still increasing. You don't have to rush it. You don't have to manufacture it. You simply have to stay close to Jesus and let the Spirit do His work.

Progress, Not Perfection

If we're honest, most of us want sanctification to be neat, tidy, and predictable. We want a graph that always trends upward. A checklist we can complete. However, spiritual growth rarely unfolds in that manner. It looks like progress and setbacks. It appears to be a combination of sudden breakthroughs and long periods of waiting. It appears to be a mix of joy and frustration. It looks like tears in the presence of God and laughter at your own weakness. It's human. It's holy. It's ongoing. And God is not measuring you against anyone else's pace. He's not comparing your journey to someone else's Instagram testimony. He's not surprised by how long it's taking. He's not disappointed that you're not "there" yet. He's walking with you. Patiently. Powerfully. Faithfully.

"The Lord is compassionate and gracious, slow to anger, abounding in love. He will not always accuse, nor will he harbor his anger forever; he does not treat us as our sins deserve or repay us according to our iniquities." Psalm 103:8–10

That's the kind of Father who is sanctifying you.

Keep Saying Yes

There will be days you feel stuck. Days you feel like you're going backward. Days you wonder if you're growing at all.

But every "yes" matters.

- Every time you choose humility over pride.

- Every time you confess instead of conceal.

- Every time you pray instead of panic.

- Every time you rest instead of strive.

- Every time you trust instead of fear.

These small moments add up. They shape you. They change you. They form Christ in you.

Letting Go of the Mask

I used to wear a mask, and maybe you've worn one too. The mask that says, *"I'm okay."* The one that hides your questions, your fears, your inconsistencies. The one that keeps you performing in public and crying in private, or just simply hardens your heart. But masks don't heal people. They isolate them. And the Holy Spirit doesn't work through the image we're projecting. He works in the truth we're willing to confess.

"If we walk in the light, as he is in the light, we have fellowship with one another, and the blood of Jesus, his Son, purifies us from all sin." 1 John 1:7

So be in the light. Let the people around you see a real, honest, and growing believer, not a perfect one. Let them see what grace looks like in real life. That's how we help each other grow.

It's Okay to Be in Process

One of the most freeing things I've learned in recent years is this: it's okay to be in process. God is not in a hurry with you. He is not ashamed of your progress. He is not surprised by your struggle. He is not disillusioned by your weakness. He knows the whole story. And He's still calling you forward. He's still shaping your heart. He's still refining your character. He's still healing what's broken.

He's still sanctifying you. And the work He's doing—though often unseen—is more powerful, more beautiful, and more eternal than you can imagine.

An Invitation to Rest

I want to leave you with the same passage that shifted everything for me, because it holds a key that many believers never find:

"There remains, then, a Sabbath-rest for the people of God; for anyone who enters God's rest also rests from their works, just as God did from his. Let us, therefore, make every effort to enter that rest..." Hebrews 4:9–11a

Make every effort... to rest. Not to prove yourself. Not to perform better. Not to finish first. But to trust deeply. To surrender consistently. To rest confidently in the finished work of Christ. Because when you rest, the Holy Spirit begins to do what striving never could. He renews your mind. He heals your heart. He convicts, comforts, restores, and empowers. And little by little—day by day—you are transformed.

Permission

My hope in writing this book wasn't to give you another checklist, but to give you permission.

- Permission to rest in the grace of God.

- Permission to stop performing and start abiding.

- Permission to admit that you're still becoming—and that's okay.

- Permission to trust the Holy Spirit with your transformation.

I'm still becoming too. And I've never been more at peace. So walk with Jesus. Keep surrendering. Keep trusting. Keep showing up. He's not finished with you yet. But He's already begun something beautiful. And He will complete it. So, friend, as you go forward, remember this:

- You are free to be in process.

- You are not alone.

- You are not who you were.

- And you are not yet who you will be.

- But you are becoming.

- You are bringing heaven to earth—one surrendered step at a time.

Let the Spirit lead. Let grace cover. And let love be your legacy. You are still becoming, and that's exactly where you're supposed to be.

In the Next Chapter...

We'll examine how our newfound freedom in the process of sanctification leads us to give more grace to others.

CHAPTER 18

GRACE FOR OTHERS — RELEASING JUDGMENT AND WALKING IN COMPASSION

One of the most surprising gifts that comes with understanding sanctification is this: it sets us free, not just from guilt and shame, but from the need to judge others. When we truly grasp that sanctification is a process and that God is gently and patiently working in us over time, we begin to see that He is doing the same in others. And just as we need grace for our own journey, we begin to extend grace to others for theirs.

The Trap of Judgment

Many Christians don't mean to be judgmental. However, when we believe that sanctification should be instantaneous, we unconsciously expect people to act perfectly the moment they say yes to Jesus. We get frustrated when a new believer still uses rough language. We wonder why someone still struggles with addiction, fear, or anger. We start placing timelines on people's growth—*"They've been a Christian for three years! Why are they still doing that?"* But spiritual growth doesn't follow our schedules and sanctification is rarely visible on the outside in its early stages. We may not see what God is doing, but He is at work. Jesus warned against this tendency to judge:

"Do not judge, or you too will be judged. For in the same way you judge others, you will be judged, and with the measure you use, it will be measured to you." Matthew 7:1–2

This wasn't just a command to be kind; it was a warning about spiritual pride. When we judge others harshly, we invite the same scrutiny into our own lives. However, when we recall how patient God has been with us, it alters our perspective on others. As we talked about earlier, if we don't have to merit our salvation, then we don't have to compare ourselves to others. If we don't have to compare ourselves to others, then we don't have to judge them; we can just love them. There are individuals who consider it their calling to judge their brothers and sisters in Christ and they do it as a "ministry" through their podcasts. I've heard of a missionary "team leader" in Thailand who claimed to have the "gift" of criticism. He spent far too much of his time doing just that—demoralizing his team. The only example of that ministry in Scripture is the Pharisees. Jesus warned us to beware of that trap.

"'Be careful,' Jesus said to them. 'Be on your guard against the yeast of the Pharisees and Sadducees.'" Matthew 16:6

Jesus and the Woman Caught in Adultery

One of the clearest examples of grace over judgment is in John 8:

"The teachers of the law and the Pharisees brought in a woman caught in adultery. They made her stand before the group and said to Jesus, 'Teacher, this woman was caught in the act of adultery. In the Law Moses commanded us to stone such women. Now what do you say?'" John 8:3–5

Jesus didn't ignore the sin. He acknowledged it. But instead of responding with condemnation, He turned the spotlight onto the hearts of the accusers:

"Let any one of you who is without sin be the first to throw a stone at her." (v. 7)

No one threw a stone. And Jesus, the only one who could have judged her righteously, said:

"'Then neither do I condemn you,' Jesus declared. 'Go now and leave your life of sin.'" (v. 11)

He offered both grace and truth—freedom from judgment and a call to transformation.

When You Understand the Process, You'll Offer More Patience

Real-life examples are everywhere:

- A young Christian at church is still learning how to control their temper. Instead of correcting them sharply, you begin to pray for them and encourage their growth.

- A person you respect as a believer makes a poor decision. Rather than gossiping about their failure, you check in, offer compassion, and let them know you're in their corner.

- A friend backslides and disappears from church for months. When they finally show up again, instead of saying, *"Where have you been?"* you say, *"I'm so glad you're here."*

This kind of posture doesn't come naturally. It comes from remembering our own journey.

Paul reminds us:

"Accept the one whose faith is weak, without quarreling over disputable matters." Romans 14:1

"You, then, why do you judge your brother or sister? Or why do you treat them with contempt? For we will all stand before God's judgment seat." Romans 14:10

If we're honest, most of us want grace for ourselves and justice for others. However, when we understand sanctification, we begin to desire grace for everyone.

Grace Creates Safe Spaces for Growth

When we walk in grace, we create environments where people can be honest, confess, struggle, and grow without fear of condemnation. This is what the Church is meant to be.

"Carry each other's burdens, and in this way you will fulfill the law of Christ." Galatians 6:2

"Be completely humble and gentle; be patient, bearing with one another in love." Ephesians 4:2

Grace makes room for sanctification. Judgment shuts it down. The more I've embraced the process of sanctification in my own life, the more I've learned to celebrate progress in others—even if they're not where I think they "should" be. Why? Because God isn't finished with them either.

Final Encouragement

Don't just receive grace. Become a dispenser of it. Let the grace you've received overflow into your relationships. Let it soften your assumptions. Let it reshape your reactions. Let it remind you that everyone is growing and that the same Spirit who is patient with you is also patient with them.

As Paul wrote:

"Therefore, as God's chosen people, holy and dearly loved, clothe yourselves with compassion, kindness, humility, gentleness and patience." Colossians 3:12

Sanctification is personal, but it was never meant to be private. Your understanding of grace can become someone else's breakthrough. Your patience can become someone else's freedom. So take off the judge's robe, put on compassion, and let God finish what He started—in you and in them.

In the Next Chapter...

We return to the beginning, the Garden of Eden, to find the conclusion.

CHAPTER 19

IN CONCLUSION – LIVING BETWEEN TWO TREES

Sanctification, the ongoing process of becoming more like Christ, is not just about behavior or theology. At its core, it's about choosing which tree we live from. In the Garden of Eden, God placed two trees at the center: the Tree of Life and the Tree of the Knowledge of Good and Evil. The first offered life through a relationship. The second offered the illusion of life, through self-reliance and moral independence. The serpent tempted Eve to eat from the Tree of the Knowledge of Good and Evil by casting doubt on God's goodness:

"Did God really say, 'You must not eat from any tree in the garden?'" Genesis 3:1

It's the same lie he still uses: *God is holding out on you. You can't fully trust Him.* It's the same doubt he used on Jesus in the wilderness:

"If you are the Son of God..." Luke 4:3

In both temptations, Satan questions identity and God's love. He knows that if he can get us to doubt both who we are and who God is, then he can lead us to reach for control—to take our sanctification into our own hands. And that's what the Tree of the Knowledge of Good and Evil represents: self-effort. It's the striving to "be like God" without trusting God. It's the exhausting pursuit of morality and perfection in our own strength. The Tree of Life, however, points to Jesus:

"I am the way and the truth and the life..." John 14:6

To eat from the Tree of Life is to rest in Christ. It's to trust that His Spirit is at work in us, not because we are good, but because He is. It's to surrender our need for control and to embrace the mystery of growth through dependence.

This Tree of Life appears again and again in Scripture. In Ezekiel's vision of the river flowing from the temple—representing the Holy Spirit—trees line the banks:

"Fruit trees of all kinds will grow on both banks of the river. Their leaves will not wither, nor will their fruit fail. Every month they will bear fruit, because the water from the sanctuary flows to them. Their fruit will serve for food and their leaves for healing." Ezekiel 47:12

And in the final chapter of Revelation:

"On each side of the river stood the tree of life, bearing twelve crops of fruit, yielding its fruit every month. And the leaves of the tree are for the healing of the nations." Revelation 22:2

Wherever the Spirit flows, the Tree of Life flourishes. Wherever we abide in Christ, fruit is inevitable—one for every season, month by month. If we stay rooted in Him, even when we feel barren, the Spirit continues to work.

It is interesting that Ezekiel saw multiple trees and John in Revelation saw only one tree, but on both sides of the river. I believe this picture is significant as we consider sanctification. As the Holy Spirit, the life-blood of Jesus, flows into us, we become like the Tree of Life.

We become replications of Jesus. We also become one with Jesus, so it becomes difficult to express whether there is one tree or many trees. It reminds me of an aspen tree forest. The largest living organism in the world is an aspen tree forest in Colorado, near Crested Butte. It is the largest living organism because scientists have discovered that, underground, the roots are all connected. They share nutrients with one another – just like we bear the fruit of life by joining ourselves to *the* Tree of Life. Jesus said:

"Remain in me, as I also remain in you. No branch can bear fruit by itself; it must remain in the vine... If you remain in me and I in you, you will bear much fruit; apart from me you can do nothing." John 15:4–5

Self-effort can only produce frustration. Trusting in Christ produces fruit. So we must ask ourselves daily: Which tree am I eating from?

- Am I trusting in God's goodness—or questioning it?

- Am I trying to become like God, or receiving who I already am in Him?

- Am I striving to prove my identity, or resting in the truth that I'm already adopted?

Sanctification is the daily decision to walk away from the Tree of Knowledge and to return to the Tree of Life. It's choosing trust over doubt, rest over striving, and Jesus over self. And when we do, the Holy Spirit does what only He can do—He makes us more like Jesus, from the inside out.

"Those who are led by the Spirit of God are the children of God." Romans 8:14

Let us live from the Tree of Life. Let us remain in Jesus. Let us become who we were always meant to be—rooted in grace, bearing fruit in season, and fully alive in Him.

AFFIRMATIONS OF MY IDENTITY IN CHRIST JESUS

Speaking Truth Over Your Life

The words we believe shape the lives we live. Many of us carry old lies—about our worth, our identity, and our place in the world—that have taken root deep within our hearts. These lies may have come from painful experiences, hurtful words, or past failures; but they do not have the final say. God's truth does. When we declare who we are in Christ, we begin to tear down these strongholds and replace them with the firm foundation of His Word. Speaking these truths aloud isn't just positive thinking—it's spiritual warfare. As you declare what God says about you, you align your mind with His perspective, renew your heart with His promises, and open the door to freedom, healing, and transformation. These affirmations are more than words—they are weapons to reclaim your identity, one truth at a time.

- I am God's beloved child, chosen and adopted into His family. (Ephesians 1:5)

- I am a new creation; my old life is gone, and my new life has begun. (2 Corinthians 5:17)

- I am redeemed and forgiven through the blood of Jesus. (Ephesians 1:7)

- God has called me by name; I belong to Him. (Isaiah 43:1)

- I am fearfully and wonderfully made; God crafted me with care and purpose. (Psalm 139:14)

- I am the light of the world, shining with God's truth and love. (Matthew 5:14)

- I am more than a conqueror through Him who loves me. (Romans 8:37)

- I am sealed with the Holy Spirit, a guarantee of my eternal inheritance. (Ephesians 1:13–14)

- I am God's workmanship, created in Christ Jesus for good works. (Ephesians 2:10)

- I am a friend of God; He has shared His heart with me. (John 15:15)

- I am deeply rooted and established in God's love. (Ephesians 3:17)

- I am the temple of the Holy Spirit; God dwells within me. (1 Corinthians 6:19)

- I am seated with Christ in the heavenly realms, far above every power. (Ephesians 2:6)

- I am chosen, holy, and dearly loved. (Colossians 3:12)

- I am justified freely by God's grace through faith in Jesus. (Romans 3:24)

- I am being transformed into the image of Christ with ever-increasing glory. (2 Corinthians 3:18)

- I am hidden in God with Christ—secure and safe. (Colossians 3:3)

- I am never alone—God is with me always, even to the end of the age. (Matthew 28:20)

- I am an ambassador of Christ, representing His kingdom on earth. (2 Corinthians 5:20)

- I am strong in the Lord and in the power of His might. (Ephesians 6:10)

GROUP STUDY QUESTIONS

Why These Questions Matter

Sanctification is personal, but it was never meant to be private. We grow best in community—with people who listen, challenge, encourage, and walk alongside us. These group study questions are designed to help you reflect more deeply, share more honestly, and grow more intentionally with others. As you talk through each chapter, you'll find that your journey is not as lonely as it sometimes feels. This is your chance to practice grace, to build trust, and to discover how powerful it is when believers sharpen one another in love. Don't rush the process—lean in, be real, and let community become part of your transformation.

Chapter 1: New Creation, Old Habitss

1. **Reflection Question:** The chapter talks about how many Christians expect instant change after salvation, but they still find themselves struggling. Looking at 2 Corinthians 5:17 and Romans 7, how can we hold the tension between being a "new creation" and still living with old habits? Can you share an instance where you've personally felt this tension?

2. **Application Question:** In the chapter, the author describes three harmful responses to struggle: faking it, feeling ashamed, and trying harder. Which of these are you most tempted to fall into and why? What would it look like for you to invite God's grace into that response instead?

3. **Community Challenge/Encouragement:** The text suggests that being honest about our process (rather than performing perfectly) can actually help those around us. How might being more transparent about your own sanctification journey encourage or free others? Is there someone whom you could be more open with this week? Is there anything that you should be more honest about with the group you're sharing with right now?

Chapter 2: Saved, Being Saved, and Help Along the Way

1. **Reflection Question:** We are saved in our spirit, but our soul is still being renewed. How have you seen this play out in your own life? In what areas is the Holy Spirit still transforming your mind, will, or emotions?

2. **Application Question:** The Holy Spirit is not only present but actively helping in our sanctification. In what ways can you become more aware of His help in your daily choices and internal battles?

3. **Community Challenge/Encouragement:** Paul reminds us that although the spirit is willing, the flesh is weak. How does understanding the difference between your spirit and soul free you from condemnation? How does it increase your dependence on God? With these answers in mind, pray for one another.

Chapter 3: God Sees the End from the Beginning

1. **Reflection Question:** This chapter describes how God sees us from an eternal perspective while we experience life moment by moment. How does knowing God "sees the end from the beginning" (Isaiah 46:10) change how you see your current struggles or failures?

2. **Application Question:** The chapter discusses the dangers of temporal thinking, such as judging ourselves based on today's struggles. What are some practical ways you could remind yourself of God's eternal perspective when you feel discouraged about your pace of growth?

3. **Community Challenge/Encouragement:** Ephesians 1:13–14 reminds us that we are marked with a seal, guaranteeing our inheritance. How could this truth help you encourage someone else who feels like they are "failing" in their spiritual walk? Who in this group today needs prayer and encouragement to move from an identity of failure to victor? Pray for one another now.

Chapter 4: The Power of the Holy Spirit

1. **Reflection Question:** The chapter describes how the Holy Spirit is not just an abstract force, but a Person who actively transforms us. How would your day-to-day spiritual walk change if you truly saw the Holy Spirit as a personal and intimately present Helper, rather than a distant power?

2. **Application Question:** Jesus said we must "remain in the Vine" (John 15:5) and Paul said to "walk by the Spirit" (Galatians 5:16). What might "remaining" and "walking" look like for you in a practical, daily sense? Can you think of a routine or habit you might add or change to stay more connected?

3. **Community Challenge/Encouragement:** This chapter highlights the distinction between serving or performing for God and living in His presence. When have you felt trapped in spiritual performance rather than dependence? How could you invite the Spirit to free you from that cycle this week? As a group, practice "abiding" together. After a moment of prayer or worship, spend 2, 5, or 10 minutes in silence, focusing on Jesus and listening to the Holy Spirit; or you can focus on a specific Scripture that has stood out. Discuss anything you saw, heard, or felt during that time as the Holy Spirit ministers to your spirit.

Chapter 5: Daily Dying, Daily Rising

1. **Reflection Question:** Jesus said we must "take up our cross daily" (Luke 9:23). What personal areas—desires, attitudes, or habits—feel most difficult for you to surrender daily? Why do you think those are hardest to let go of?

2. **Application Question:** This chapter provides practical examples of daily dying, such as forgiving someone or admitting weakness. Which of those examples challenged you the most and how could you practice it in your life this week?

3. **Community Challenge/Encouragement:** We read that "death brings life," and that the same Spirit who raised Jesus lives in us (Romans 8:11). How does this promise give you courage to keep surrendering to God, even when it feels painful or risky? Choose to surrender those things again today in a prayerful agreement as a group.

Chapter 6: Renewing the Mind

1. **Reflection Question:** The chapter describes how "behavior is the fruit, but belief is the root." Which of the six examples of hidden beliefs resonated most with you? Is there another hidden belief that God brought to your attention as you read this section? Why do you think that particular belief has been hard to replace with truth?

2. **Application Question:** Romans 12:2 calls us to, "be transformed by the renewing of your mind." What is one lie you feel the Holy Spirit is inviting you to replace with truth this week? If you're not sure, pause now and ask Him to show you a lie you're believing currently. Ask God to give you a Scripture with the Truth to replace that lie and meditate on that Truth this week.

3. **Community Challenge/Encouragement:** The author shares about family wounds shaping his view of God as a Father. How might sharing your own story of distorted beliefs—and God's healing—encourage someone else to pursue renewing their mind? Share a story with the group today that could bring encouragement to someone else and freedom to yourself.

Chapter 7: Putting On the New Self

1. **Reflection Question:** This chapter talks about "putting on the new self" as a daily, intentional choice. What old habits or patterns do you still find yourself tempted to put back on? What new practices could you intentionally replace them with?

2. **Application Question:** The chapter describes the difference between "trying" and "training" (1 Timothy 4:7–8). What is one spiritual discipline you could start practicing this month as part of your "training" in godliness? How might you build support or accountability around it?

3. **Community Challenge/Encouragement:** Paul reminds us that our identity ("holy and dearly loved") comes before our behavior. How does remembering this order help you face moments when you don't "feel" holy or new? Can you think of a time recently when you needed to cling to that truth? Is there an area concerning your identity today where you need encouragement from the group to help you walk in truth instead of a lie? Share that issue and invite the others in the group to speak truth into it.

Chapter 8: Sanctification and Spiritual Epigenetics

1. **Reflection Question:** This chapter compares your spiritual DNA to a seed in different types of soil (Matthew 13). What "soil conditions" in your current environment might be helping or hindering the expression of Christ's nature in you?

2. **Application Question:** The text describes how media, relationships, and culture shape our spiritual environment. What is one intentional change you could make this week to improve your "soil," and how might that help your growth in Christ?

3. **Community Challenge/Encouragement:** James 5:16 states that healing comes through honest confession in community. What makes it hard for you to be vulnerable with trusted believers? What would help you take a step toward that kind of grace-filled relationship? Ask God for courage and confess any hidden sins (such as gossip, unforgiveness, or fear) to the group today, and then pray for one another (James 5:16).

Chapter 9: Trusting and Resting

1. **Reflection Question:** The chapter describes how true and proper rest requires trust. In what areas of your life do you struggle most to let go of control and trust God? What fears or beliefs might be keeping you from resting in Him?

2. **Application Question:** Hebrews 4 calls us to, "make every effort to enter that rest." What practical steps could you take this week to move from striving to abiding? For example, how might you slow down, simplify, or build in moments to remember God's promises?

3. **Community Challenge/Encouragement:** This chapter highlights the difference between relating to Jesus as Lord compared to just a teacher. How does seeing Him as your Lord—rather than merely a wise example—shape your ability to rest in His finished work? What might change if you truly trusted Him as Lord? Share with the group any struggles you may be having in this area. Don't fear being judged. Be honest and trust God to help you. Shake off hypocrisy and get real with one another.

Chapter 10: Peter — From Passion to Hypocrisy to Restoration

1. **Reflection Question:** Peter's failures were dramatic and public, yet Jesus restored him with love instead of shame. How does Peter's story challenge or encourage you in your own moments of failure?

2. **Application Question:** Peter struggled with people-pleasing and fear, even after years of following Jesus. Which areas in your own life might be vulnerable to "back sliding," and how can you invite God's grace into those areas today?

3. **Community Challenge/Encouragement:** Peter accepted correction (even public correction) as part of his sanctification. How willing are you to receive corrections from others? What steps could you take to grow in humility and openness to that process? If you are ready, ask others in the group to be honest with you and correct you as needed today. Be humble and take every suggestion before the Lord, remembering that you are loved and not judged because of Jesus' finished work on the cross. Don't allow yourself to be offended. Trust the good intentions of those who share with you, even if you disagree with them in the end.

Chapter 11: Paul and John Mark — Growth on Both Sides

1. **Reflection Question:** Think about Paul and Barnabas's "sharp disagreement" over John Mark (Acts 15). How does their conflict encourage you to see that even mature believers can disagree and still be used by God?

2. **Application Question:** Both John Mark and Paul grew through this relational tension. Who in your life might God be using to shape you, even through conflict or disappointment? How could you approach that relationship differently in light of this story?

3. **Community Challenge/Encouragement:** Paul eventually called Mark "helpful" again. Is there someone you've given up on—maybe even yourself—who might need another chance? How could you extend grace and encouragement to them this week? If that relationship is with someone in this group, have an open and loving discussion today, forgiving one another and giving each other grace to "be in the process."

Chapter 12: Apollos — The Power of Humble Growth

1. **Reflection Question:** Apollos was passionate, knowledgeable, and bold, yet still needed correction. How does his story challenge your view of spiritual maturity? Where might you need to stay teachable, even if you feel confident?

2. **Application Question:** Priscilla and Aquila corrected Apollos gently and relationally. How could you follow their example if you see someone in your community with an incomplete or imbalanced understanding of the faith?

3. **Community Challenge/Encouragement:** Apollos didn't let pride block his growth. Is there an area where you feel resistant to correction or feedback right now? What would it look like to invite someone you trust to help you grow there? Share with the group where you feel resistant and allow them to speak into that area (remembering that God resists the proud, but gives grace to those who humble themselves).

Chapter 13: Mary Magdalene — From Darkness to Devotion

1. **Reflection Question:** Mary Magdalene was delivered from deep spiritual bondage, yet became one of Jesus' most faithful followers. What areas of your life has Jesus already brought freedom to? How can that history fuel deeper devotion today?

2. **Application Question:** Even after following Jesus closely, Mary misunderstood the resurrection and assumed the worst. Can you think of a time when confusion or grief clouded your understanding of what God was doing? How did He gently meet you in that moment?

3. **Community Challenge/Encouragement:** Jesus entrusted Mary with the first proclamation of His resurrection. What does this reveal about how Jesus values people, especially those still in process? How might God be calling you to share your testimony, even if you feel unfinished? Share something personal with the group today about what God is doing in you now and where you are at in the process of sanctification.

Chapter 14: Free to Be in Process

1. **Reflection Question:** This chapter challenges us to be vulnerable and "free to be in process." What fears or beliefs have kept you from being honest about your struggles with others? What might happen if you brought those into the light?

2. **Application Question:** You read that vulnerability creates safety for others. Who in your life might need you to go first, in sharing something real and tangible, so that they can feel free to do the same? How could you take that step this week?

3. **Community Challenge/Encouragement:** Imagine a church where it's safe to struggle, where leaders admit weakness, and where grace flows freely. What practical changes do you think your own church or community group would need to make to look more like that vision? Practice those suggestions within your group now. Remember that we are the church, so the change starts with each one of us.

Chapter 15: Grace Over Guilt

1. **Reflection Question:** Think about a time when you felt guilt after failing spiritually. How did that guilt impact your relationship with God? How might it have looked different if you had responded with grace-fueled conviction instead?

2. **Application Question:** The chapter states that grace is a *present power*, not just a past event or a future hope. What would it look like for you to approach God's throne of grace "with confidence" this week in a real area of struggle? Start now.

3. **Community Challenge/Encouragement:** Why do you think some churches or believers rely on guilt as a motivator rather than grace? How could we help one another shift from a guilt-based spirituality to a grace-based transformation within our communities? Practice together, coming up with ideas on how to confront sin with grace instead of guilt. How can you respond to someone stuck in an addiction, in gossip, in unforgiveness, etc?

Chapter 16: Heaven on Earth — A Sanctified Life

1. **Reflection Question:** Which fruit of the Spirit from Galatians 5:22–23 do you see most evident in your life right now, and which one do you feel the Holy Spirit is inviting you into the process of cultivating more intentionally?

2. **Application Question:** The chapter describes how a sanctified life is not about drawing attention to yourself, but about pointing others to Jesus. What is one area of your life that you can invite God's love into so that you are not a "resounding gong or a clanging cymbal?" Pray now and ask God to bring His love into that area of your life.

3. **Community Challenge/Encouragement:** How might your understanding of sanctification change if you truly saw it as revealing *Christ in you* rather than improving *you*? Share any ways this perspective might affect your relationships, priorities, or even your self-talk.

Chapter 17: I'm Still Becoming

1. **Reflection Question:** In what area of your life do you most struggle to believe *"I am still becoming"* instead of *"I should already be there?"* How might God be inviting you to rest and trust Him in that place right now?

2. **Application Question:** The chapter describes "letting go of the mask" and living in the light. What would it look like for you to be more honest about your struggles with a trusted friend or your community this week?

3. **Community Challenge/Encouragement:** How does understanding that, *"sanctification is a process, not a performance,"* change the way you see yourself—and the way you see others who are also on the journey? Ask forgiveness from the people you have been judging and consider sharing with them where you are in the process of sanctification, especially the people in this group.

Chapter 18: Grace for Others — Releasing Judgment and Walking in Compassion

1. **Reflection Question:** How has your understanding of your *own* sanctification journey changed your view of the struggles or failures of others? Can you think of a time when you judged someone too quickly?

2. **Application Question:** This chapter discusses creating "safe spaces for growth" within your community. What is one practical way you can help make your church, small group, or home a place where others feel safe to be honest and grow?

3. **Community Challenge/Encouragement:** Jesus offered the woman caught in adultery both grace and truth. How can you personally balance grace and truth in your relationships without leaning too far toward harsh judgment and without ignoring sin? Share with the group an example of when you were driven too much by grace or truth.

Chapter 19: In Conclusion - Living Between Two Trees

1. **Reflection Question:** In what areas of your life are you most tempted to "eat from the Tree of the Knowledge of Good and Evil"—trying to fix, control, or perfect yourself instead of trusting God?

2. **Application Question:** The Tree of Life represents trust and dependence on Jesus. Practically speaking, what could it look like this week for you to *abide* in Him rather than striving in your own strength?

3. **Community Challenge/Encouragement:** Revelation pictures the Tree of Life as bringing healing to the nations. How might your personal choice to live from the Tree of Life (trusting God and depending on the Spirit) influence or bring healing to the people around you? Your family? This group? Share with the group one current circumstance where you realize you have been responding from the Tree of Knowledge of Good and Evil and ask the others for ideas of how to respond in this circumstance from the Tree of Life.

WORKS CITED

Aboud, Nora M., et. al. "Genetics, Epigenetic Mechanism." *National Library of Medicine*, 14 Aug. 2023, https://ncbi.nlm.nih.gov/books/NBK532999/

Ginsburg, J.A. "Flickers of Change: Epigenetics, Cymatics, & Regeneration." *Medium*, 14 Feb. 2022, https://jaginsburg.medium.com/flickers-of-change-epigenetics-cymatics-regeneration-d51da6dc6d4f

"Jehovah Rapha." *Strong's Exhaustive Concordance: King James Version Bible, Bible Hub Online Version*, http://biblehub.com/hebrew/7495.htm. Accessed 5 July 2025.

Lieberman, Matthew D., et al. "Putting Feelings into Words: Affect Labeling Disrupts Amygdala Activity in Response to Affective Stimuli." *Psychological science* vol. 18,5 (2007): 421-8. doi:10.1111/j.1467-9280.2007.01916.x

"Raphah." *Strong's Exhaustive Concordance: King James Version Bible, Bible Hub Online Version*, https://biblehub.com/hebrew/7495.htm. Accessed 5 July 2025.